Twayne's English Authors Series

Sylvia Bowman, *Editor*

INDIANA UNIVERSITY

Walter de la Mare

(TEAS) 33

Walter de la Mare

By DORIS ROSS McCROSSON

Wilson College

Twayne Publishers, Inc.   ::   New York

For S. Edward Hannestad

Preface

IN THIS SHORT critical-analytical study of the writings of Walter de la Mare, I have attempted to do two things. First, I have concentrated on his novels because I feel that in them one finds the clearest statement of his vision of life. It is the novels, however, that have been most neglected; and even when not ignored, they have been, I think, misinterpreted. I hope my reading of them will help to illuminate the poetry and short stories.

Second, I have gone to his poetry and short stories with what I hope is a fresh approach. I am aware of much of the criticism written about de la Mare's work in these genres, but I have not relied to any great extent upon other readings. I have instead approached the works themselves in an attempt to dispel the unfortunate idea held by most Americans who have any familiarity with de la Mare—that he is primarily a children's writer. Of course, much of his poetry and prose was written expressly for children; but to consider him primarily a writer for children is to do him a grave injustice. It is this injustice I hope this study will help rectify.

It is my purpose to trace the ways in which de la Mare searched for meaning in his short stories, his poetry, and his novels. To do so, I have first discussed his speculations concerning the nature of the imagination and of dreams. These discussions, I hope, will illuminate the ensuing considerations of his work. In the last chapter, I summarize what I believe to be his achievement and attempt to assess his contribution to literature. I wish to express my thanks to The Society of Authors for permission to quote from the works of Mr. de la Mare.

DORIS ROSS McCROSSON

Wilson College
May, 1965

Contents

Contents

Chronology

Walter de la Mare's outward life was singularly and refreshingly uneventful. Of few others can it be said with equal truth that his adventures were in his imagination. The significant events in his life and his major publications are cited below.

April 25, 1873.   Born at Charlton in Kent; son of James Edward Delamare and Lucy Sophia Browning Delamare. Educated at St. Paul's Cathedral Choir School in London where he founded at sixteen the school magazine, *The Choristers' Journal*. He was editor of nine issues to which he probably contributed most of the material.

1890   Unable to go to college, de la Mare became a bookkeeper in the London offices of the Anglo-American (Standard) Oil Company.

1895   First appearance in print (except for his schoolboy venture): "Kismet" in *The Sketch*.

1899   Married to Constance Elfrida Igpen, who died in 1943. The de la Mares had four children: two sons and two daughters.

1902   First book published, a collection of poems: *Songs of Childhood*, under the pseudonym "Walter Ramal."

1904   *Henry Brocken*, the first of the long prose fiction, was published. On the title page appeared for the first time his real name.

1908   Granted a Civil List pension of a hundred pounds annually by the Asquith government. He retired from business to devote himself entirely to writing.

1910   Two novels, *The Return* and *The Three Mulla-Mulgars* (later reprinted as *The Three Royal Monkeys*), were published.

1912   *The Listeners and Other Poems* published. Although a previous volume of poems (other than *Songs of Childhood*) had appeared in 1906, as well as many single poems in magazines, this volume established Mr. de la Mare's reputation.

1919   *Rupert Brooke and the Intellectual Imagination*, a lecture; subsequently reprinted in *Pleasures and Speculations* (1940), an important collection of essays.

1920   *Poems 1901 to 1918*. Includes most of his previously published poems.

1921   *Memoirs of a Midget* published. Considered to be his finest novel.

1923   *Come Hither*, the first of de la Mare's anthologies; collects rhymes and poems "for young people of all ages."

1925   *Broomsticks and Other Tales*, a collection of twelve short stories for children.

1928   *At First Sight*, called "a novel" by de la Mare. This was to be his last novel.

1930   *Desert Islands and Robinson Crusoe* published. An unusual, fascinating book about travel lore.

1935   *Early One Morning in the Spring*. Sub-titled "Chapters on children and childhood as it is revealed in particular in early memories and early writings," this work can be called an anthology; but the personal tone of its observations identifies it as a significant contribution to autobiographical literature.

1935   *Poems 1919 to 1934.*

1939   *Behold, This Dreamer!*, an anthology, again unique, subtitled, "Of reverie, night, sleep, dream, love-dreams, nightmare, death, the unconscious, the imagination, divination, the artist, and kindred subjects."

1942   *Collected Poems.*

1942   *Best Stories of Walter de la Mare*, a selection made by the author.

1945   *The Burning Glass and other poems . . . including The Traveller*. The American edition, published by Viking Press. The London edition does not include *The Traveller*.

1948   Made a Companion of Honor.

1953   Received the Order of Merit. Other honors accorded during his later life include: Hon. D. Litt., Oxford; Hon. Litt. D., Cambridge; Hon. LL.D., St. Andrews; Hon. D. Litt., Bristol and London; Hon. Fellow, Keble College, Oxford.

June 22, 1956.   Died at home in Twickenham.

CHAPTER 1

The Shaping Spirit

ONCE, almost half facetiously, Walter de la Mare suggested that England's climate may account for the variety and richness of the English imagination.[1] He often speculated upon the imagination, its origin, and its capabilities; but only in the lecture "Rupert Brooke and the Intellectual Imagination" delivered in 1919 did he attempt, and not entirely successfully, to analyze it. This lecture is not successful possibly because his subject was, primarily, Rupert Brooke, but also because analysis seemed uncongenial to de la Mare. Then, too, as he demonstrates in his anthologies, his own imagination was so lively that he was not at his best when he had to "stick to the subject." The Rupert Brooke lecture, nevertheless, provides a basis for an understanding of de la Mare's concept of the imagination; and, although he directs his remarks specifically to the poetic imagination, what he has to say can easily be applied to imagination in general.

He finds that there are two predominant types of imagination: the childlike and the boylike. Those who have a childlike imagination are like all children: "They are not so closely confined and bound in by their groping senses. Facts to them are the liveliest of chameleons. Between their dreams and their actuality looms no impassable abyss. There is no solitude more secluded . . . no absorption more complete, no perception more exquisite, and one might even add, more comprehensive. . . . They are contemplatives, solitaries, fakirs, who sink again and again out of the noise and fever of existence into a waking vision."[2] Children are, in short, visionaries. As they mature, however, what is childlike "retires like a shocked snail into its shell . . . consciousness from being chiefly subjective becomes largely objective." It is at this point that the "boyish type of mind and imagination, the intellectual, analytical type begins . . . to flourish."[3]

By the time the boy has grown to manhood, his imagination has been molded by either one or the other phase. In other words, the "shocked snail" either remains permanently in its shell or it refuses to be intimidated by actuality and continues to roam at will. If the latter occurs and the childlike persists, the adult's imagination is visionary; it is "intuitive, inductive." But, if his mind is shaped by boyhood, his imagination will be intellectual, or "logical, deductive." Making a nice distinction here, de la Mare shows the difference between the visionary imagination and the intellectual: "The one knows that beauty is truth, the other reveals that truth is beauty." [4] It is the difference between a Plato, Plotinus, Vaughan, Blake, or Yeats, and a Lucretius, Dryden, Pope, Byron, Browning, Meynell, or Brooke.

Although de la Mare recognizes, of course, that even the most objective and analytic of minds is occasionally likely to daydream and to have intuitive insights and that, conversely, the childlike, visionary mind is occasionally supremely matter-of-fact, his distinctions are helpful.[5] We cannot argue with his contention that the greatest poets—Shakespeare, Dante, Goethe—possessed equally both types of imagination; although we might do so when de la Mare finds Keats, as well as Wordsworth and Eliot, on the "borderland" between the two.

Another distinction de la Mare draws between the two types concerns their sources of poetry: the visionary's are within, while the intellectual's are without—in action, knowledge of things, and experience. The result is that, in the intellectual's poetry, "there is less mystery and wonder, less magic. . . . It does not demand of its reader so profound or so complete a surrender." But de la Mare does not think that it is any less good as poetry (although there is no doubt where his own preference lies); it is simply a different kind: "we can ardently welcome its courage, enthusiasm and energy . . . its penetrating thought, its wit and fervour and arrogance. . . ." [6]

The distinction de la Mare draws in this lecture between types of mind is to be found elsewhere in his prose. But the terms shift to the more conventional "reason" as opposed to "imagination" possibly to eliminate the necessity of clarifying modifiers. Ultimately, his distinction follows Coleridge, for whom "fancy" is memory and derives its material from the phenomenal world, while "imagination" transcends the senses and receives its material from the eternal.[7] De la Mare is also indebted to Coleridge for the epithet "the shaping spirit" which he often uses in reference to the imagination.

That the imagination, in the Coleridgean sense, is of paramount importance was obvious to de la Mare. Reason, he felt, apprehends matters-of-fact; the imagination, matters-of-truth: "in the realm of the imagination all things excepting the unimaginable are possible."[8] Reason itself seemed to him to depend, in part at least, upon the imagination; for "the mind . . . will do little what we wish until we have 'imagined' the wish fulfilled."[9] Furthermore, the phenomenal world is not the supreme reality because "nature itself resembles a veil over some further reality of which the imagination in its visionary moments seems to achieve a more direct evidence."[10] To rest, therefore, on knowledge gained through the senses is to depend upon appearances only.

However, there is the "underside" of the imagination to be taken into account; and de la Mare—although his scrutiny is not often very steady, it cannot be called anything less than comprehensive—recognizes that the imagination does not always deal in sweetness and light. It has its darker aspects. Evil flourishes in his fiction and is made manifest just, as he says, "imaginative evil" flourishes in the dark.[11] And the imagination is vulnerable to its depredations. Jealousy, for example, "may make its entry solely through the imagination" although he calls it a disease of the blood and body rather than of the spirit. But the fact that it can enter through the imagination is to him convincing proof of the "communion and interaction" between body and mind;[12] also, incidentally, it is proof of the sovereign power of the imagination.

It might be well to comment at this point that de la Mare does not make any consistent distinctions between the imagination, the mind, and the spirit. The terms shift. Sometimes—often, in fact—they are synonymous: they are not so clear-cut as, for example, the distinctions made by Meredith whose "blood, brains, spirit" triumvirate was to have so much influence. But, time and again, one is aware that de la Mare is delightfully consistent in his inconsistencies. He was not a scientist; what he felt true of the language of poets with a "visionary" imagination may be applied to his own: the words "seem chiefly to mean what is left hinted at, rather than expressed";[13] for, he lamented, "like the unicorn, alas, *the* word may prove to be non-existent." [14] It is equally possible, as T. S. Eliot suggested, that what de la Mare was trying to say in his fiction is beyond the power of language to express.[15] And it is more than possible that de la Mare did not have a little mind for which inconsistencies could be the hobgoblins. Whatever the reason, it is obvious that he remained true to his central idea that the imagination is the "shaping spirit" of man.

But, although he believed this wholeheartedly, de la Mare did not for the moment suggest that the artist or anyone else should retire wholly into his imagination, and his own life shows that he himself did not. "The artist who . . . enwraps himself in the solitude of his imagination may learn many secrets and attain to an esoteric knowledge of the truth that lies concealed beneath appearances"; but, at the same time, he would lose "touch and sympathy with the thoughts and desires, the loves, cares, follies of this workaday world; and dreams at last may cheat him of his goal." Conversely, he warned that, if the artist "disobeys his intuitions and gives himself even to the best of practical causes, he risks the sacrifice of the rarer imaginative truth which is in him." [16]

Whence comes the imagination? What are its sources? De la Mare is not so specific on this question as a scientist or philosopher might be, but he is highly suggestive and some of his theories are reminiscent of those of Carl Jung. Equated with the imagination, and possibly antecedent to it is the unconscious—the "reservoir of the *elixer vitae*" on which intuition and imagination draw. Indeed, the unconscious *is* for de la Mare the source of all that makes a being human. "What," he asks, "*can* man achieve, indeed, unaided by the reviving waters of this unplumbable well?" [17] Into this well go "every fusion of memory, every fancy and fantasy, dream and daydream." [18] Out of it comes all we know of reality.

But de la Mare did not think that this "unplumbable well" begins to fill upon a person's birth, or that its "reviving waters" would be drained away by death. It is here that de la Mare seems to echo Jung's theory of the collective unconscious wherein, according to Jung, rest the "primordial images common to humanity," which he calls archetypes. These are "the most ancient and the most universal 'thought-forms' of humanity," for the collective unconscious itself "is entirely universal . . . its contents can be found everywhere." [19]

De la Mare describes the unconscious as "an archipelago of humanity whose myriad island peaks are connected under the sea," [20] a metaphor he uses many times throughout his fiction. Closely paralleling Jung, de la Mare felt that in the unconscious was held "the wild and ancient stock of dream"; [21] and that the English downs embodied ancestral memories[22] although "our human tap roots . . . pierce deeper than the fibers of nationality and race." [23] And he felt that, while the unconscious "oozes secrets that are chiefly physical concerning a remote and sunken physical past," it also oozes secrets "which refer to a no less remote but spiritual future." [24]

Throughout the entire de la Mare canon the "impossible she" is the most pervasive and persistent archetype. Who "she" is exactly, one cannot know: "She is memory and strangeness, earth's delight, and death's promise. In a thousand shapes and disguises she visits us." [25] Long before critics had turned their attention to the exploration of myth and archetypes in literature, de la Mare recognized and utilized the myth of exile or banishment from what, in Christian terms, is Eden and the dwelling place of his "impossible she"; "The old Adam, the happy prehistoric child, in every one of us, . . . harks back in spirit to the garden of his banishment; wherein Eve awaits him, and he can be once more happy and at peace, the veil withdrawn, all old enmities forgiven and forgotten, amid its beauty and life." [26]

The Platonic element in de la Mare's conception of the "impossible she" is also easy to discern. Shelley's Intellectual Beauty is a near cousin, and almost equally unattainable. For Plato, when a man sees an object of beauty, he recollects the Idea of Beauty; more specifically, seeing a beautiful face awakens in him a longing for the world of the ideal wherein he lived before being born into the phenomenal world—the world of shadows. De la Mare's "impossible she" awakens in many of his characters the same unbearable longing; she is "the grave and lovely overshadowing dream whose surrender made life a torment, and death the near fold of an immortal, starry veil." [27] But surrender the dream one must, in this life at least—as does Arthur Lawford, for example, in *The Return.*

Among de la Mare's predecessors in the genre of dream literature, George MacDonald in particular utilized this theme. In *Lilith,* for example, the central character is enchanted by the beauty of Lona who assumes Platonic-archetypal characteristics: "I seem to have known her for ages—for always—from before time began. I hardly remembered my mother, but in my mind's eye she now looked like Lona; and if I imagined sister or child, invariably she had the face of Lona. My every imagination flew to her; she was my heart's wife." [28] How similar MacDonald's concept is to de la Mare's is obvious upon comparison of this passage to Arthur Lawford's plea to his "impossible she," Grisel, in *The Return:* " 'Be just the memory of my mother, the face, the friend I've never seen; the voice that every dream leaves echoing.' " [29]

But, although de la Mare's "impossible she" can be more comfortably explained as being Platonic in nature, there are in her, undoubtedly, elements of Jung's concept of the *anima.* Jung maintains that "an inherited collective image of woman exists in a man's unconscious." This universal image, or archetype, Jung identifies with the feminine aspects of a man's own nature, aspects all Western men consider it a virtue to repress. Thus, the *anima* becomes a repository for the "contra-sexual" demands born of such repression.

However, every man must recognize and come to terms with his *anima,* which can serve the function of mediator between his conscious and unconscious selves. Contemporary Western man seldom gets the opportunity to do so; his first projection of the *anima* is his mother—his "mother-imago" who protects him "from the darkness of his psyche"; who is his "safeguard against the unconscious." Merely becoming an adult does not guarantee either separation from this projection of the *anima* or recognition of it for what it is; for, instead of recognizing and dealing with the *anima* in the form of the "mother-imago," he transfers her functions to his wife. He seeks a love partner, in other words, "who best corresponds to his own unconscious femininity—a woman, in short, who can unhesitatingly receive the projection of his soul."

The results of such a marriage, Jung maintains, can be disastrous for what the man is really seeking in his wife is the protection he enjoyed as a child. A psychologically healthy man must achieve a separation from the mother as *anima* or soul image; he must

[18]

recognize his "distinction" from the *anima*. Failure to do so, Jung maintains, "failure to adapt to this inner world is a negligence entailing just as serious consequences as ignorance and ineptitude in the outer world." In order that a man "objectivate the effects of the *anima* and . . . try to understand what contents underlie those effects," he must make concessions to both the outer and inner worlds; thus he achieves what Jung, borrowing the Oriental concept of Tao, calls "the union of opposites through the middle path."[30]

It is entirely possible that de la Mare's "impossible she" is a projection of his *anima*. Certainly she has the mysterious power to evoke inexpressible longings in many of de la Mare's male characters: in *Henry Brocken*, she is Criseyde; in *The Three Mulla-Mulgars*, she is the water-midden; in *The Return*, she is Grisel; in *At First Sight*, she is Miss Simcox. And in countless numbers of the short stories and poems she plays a part; perhaps she is most aptly evoked in "The Phantom," the last stanza of which succinctly describes her:

> All the world's woods, tree o'er tree,
> Come to nought.
> Birds, flowers, beasts, how transient they,
> Angels of a flying day.
> Love is quenched; dreams drown in sleep;
> Ruin nods along the deep:
> Only thou immortally
> Hauntest on
> This poor earth in Time's flux caught;
> Hauntest on, pursued, unwon,
> Phantom child of memory,
> Beauteous one!

Who she is, de la Mare does not venture to guess. He only seemed sure that "A thousand cheating names hath she/ And none foretokens rest."[31] If, as Jung maintained, "a man brings forth his work as a complete creation out of his inner feminine nature,"[32] the "impossible she" might have been an objectivation for de la Mare of his inner nature, but unrecognized as such. She may be in Jung's terms a "relatively independent" personality who was not "integrated" into de la Mare's consciousness; he was unable to use the *anima* "purposefully" as a function because her contents remained unknown to him. It is only, Jung says, when the "conscious mind has become sufficiently familiar with the unconscious processes reflected in the anima" that the *anima* will "be felt simply as a function" of the whole personality.[33]

Whatever her identity, Platonic or Jungian, the "impossible she" was, however, one of de la Mare's chief sources of inspiration: certainly she appears as the most persistent theme. That she was a creation of his imagination, there can be no doubt. But it is important to remember that de la Mare equated the imagination with the unconscious; and, because he did, this may be the partial reason for his failure to come to terms with reality, to find a consistent core or center from which to operate. In short, he could not, or did not, come to terms with his own unconscious. The very epithet he implies to this mysterious being, the "impossible she," is enough to indicate that this was so—if one remembers that he believed that "in the realm of the imagination all things excepting the unimaginable are possible." That he could not extend his imagination to embrace a concept of a "possible she"—either as a child would "intuitively" or as a boy, "logically"—is obvious.

CHAPTER 2

Dreams and the Dreamer

CLOSELY related to de la Mare's speculations about the nature of the imagination, and possibly even more important to an understanding of his work, are his speculations about dreams. That dreams were to him something more than an inexplicable and inconsequential part of existence can be seen in his vast and infinitely fascinating compilation of literature on the subject, *Behold, This Dreamer!* (1939) which, besides a lengthy essay as an introduction to the anthology, contains accounts of experiences, speculations, poems, and observations about dreams compiled from some four hundred sources. From Homer, the Bible, and Apuleius, to C. D. Lewis, Helen Waddell, and Logan Pearsall Smith; from what is conceivably every source in English, in the original or translated, de la Mare has gleaned the literature of the Western world for this remarkable volume. Every source, that is, but one—the one which more than likely comes to most minds immediately the word "dream" is mentioned—Freud.

Far from ignoring Freud, de la Mare deals with him in the introduction to this volume and elsewhere; but in most cases he does so rather disparagingly. He tells an anecdote, for example, of a little girl's avoiding the cracks in the pavement while walking beside a "famous philosopher" who "amiably announced: 'Ah! I see you have a complex!'" De la Mare's comment is: "It would be both ignorant and irreverent to suspect him of a simplex." [1]

A "simplex" is what de la Mare accuses Freud of having, at least in relation to his theory of sexuality. De la Mare did not minimize the importance of sex, and he was not a prude; he maintained, however, that Freudianism "narrowed and adulterated" the meaning of love by focusing upon only one of its many, equally mysterious elements.[2] To de la Mare, "Sexual fruition after all is only one course in love's banquet. . . . It may satisfy awhile the body, but never, wholly the spirit." [3]

On the subject of dreams, de la Mare again seems to agree with Carl Jung who broke with Freud primarily because of what he felt was Freud's misguided attempt to reduce everything to the common denominator of sex. I have no way of knowing at this time whether de la Mare had read much of Jung; but, since he was so widely read, there seems little doubt that he had. And if he had, he would have underscored heartily Jung's discussion of Plato's myth of the cave which, Jung suggested, if we analyze in Freudian terms "we should naturally come to the uterus, and we should have proved that even the mind of Plato was deeply stuck in the primeval levels of 'infantile sexuality' "; but, Jung points out, in so doing "we should also remain in total ignorance of what Plato actually created from the primitive antecedents of his philosophical intuition." [4] This same idea de la Mare expressed more colorfully: "That a Blatant Beast, with virtues of its own nature, is confined in the cellar known as the Unconscious . . . is undeniable; but there is also a caged bird in the attic, and one of a marvelous song." [5]

He also gave short shrift to the theory that dream symbols are necessarily sex symbols; for, as he quite rightly says, "There is scarcely an object around us that cannot be conceived of as a symbol figurative of anything with which the waking mind is deeply concerned." [6] And elsewhere he shows again his impatience with this kind of dream analysis by observing that the face of a person in love "no more resembles a face transformed by the sexual than a dream of lotus flowers on a moon-lit pool resembles the Freudian interpretation of it." [7]

No better proof is there that he did not credit Freud's theory of sexuality than the fact that he recorded in several of his essays some of his own dreams—dreams so filled with overtones of lust, murder, and guilt that analysis in Freudian terms would have sent him, had he believed them valid, straight to the master himself. On yet another occasion he mocks Freudianism with devastating understatement: "What the Censor may conceal in such symbols as onions, peppercorns, gherkins, cauliflowers I dare not guess." [8] At bottom, however, what seemed to be the crux of his quarrel with Freud is that he felt that, by imposing an "arbitrary interpretation" on dreams, "they have been sacrificed not only to sex . . . but to a degraded conception of it." [9]

Dreams were far too precious and far too fascinating to de la Mare to be so dismissed or at least to be so shabbily used, for he felt that they are in a sense a communion of the self with the self.[10] He confessed that he himself had spent more time adventuring in dreams then he had while awake[11] and that his dreams profoundly influenced him.[12] In fact, he admitted, once at least in conversation, that it would have been hard for him to choose between which he preferred—dream life or waking life.[13] I almost wrote "dream life and *real* life," but de la Mare would have remarked that there was no difference, for to him imagination and dreams were practically synonymous—and both were paths to reality.

Dreams were to de la Mare the source of poetry. Inspiration seems to come in a "condition of consciousness compounded in some degree of both dream and wake," [14] in which condition poems seems to appear "like self-created phantoms." [15] Elsewhere he refers to inspiration as a "golden pause in life" when "Life is no longer a riddle but a dream," [16] and asks: "What indeed, is every work of art before it is accomplished but a day dream with a definite purpose and a particular goal?" [17]

Not only did he feel that dreams are the source of art, he was also convinced that the enjoyment of literature is largely dependent upon the reader's capacity to dream.[18] When we experience a poem, or fall in love, it is the same as when we embark upon a dream: "the whole of our world is changed"; for, when these things occur, "the spirit within us seems for the moment to have returned to a state of being and to an abode of which the earth with all its loveliness is only a partial and illusive reflection." [19]

Another aspect of dreams which fascinated de la Mare is the possibility that sleep may be the boundary which separates two or more personalities, a possibility hinted at in his suggestion that we set out in dream, as it were, "as if to keep an assignation with a friend—a second self." [20] Referring to this idea, he speculated that perhaps sleep was even another state of being, one distinct from the state of waking.[21] For, although he found that people may wish for fulfillment of their waking lives in dreams, he felt it untenable to believe that the life experienced in dreams is a mere extension of waking experience. About this point, he suggests with characteristic humor: "Life's punctual magpie serial is at least more amusing for being the work of two collaborators so unalike in style, so much at odds regarding form and matter and method, so various in their shocking disregard of our tastes and ideals; and so remote one from the other apparently in motive, value, and moral code, and in their notions of the sane, the significant, the welcome, and the useful." [22]

De la Mare also admitted the possibility that dreams may be "precognitive" and "prophetic" [23] and that they sometimes—although rarely—so closely resemble actuality that they may be relics of a previous life.[24] He even suggests that occurrences in history have a dream-like quality. Balboa, wading into the Pacific to take possession of it; Pizarro, lacking iron, shoeing his horses with gold—"Such things, however remote they may be, seem to belong to some dream life of our own, as if we had once actually participated in them!" [25]

In fact, de la Mare was prepared to admit almost any possibility concerning the origin of dreams: not only may they be the vestiges of race memories,[26] or the reminiscences of a former life,[27] they may also come from another and higher intelligence.[28] For he asks: "We say, we think; but would it be nearer the truth to say, We are thought into?" [29]

That life—awake and asleep—and death were inextricably interwoven de la Mare also seemed certain. His preoccupation with death had nothing of the morbid in it; he simply felt that death was as interesting and as curious a state as life. He could not imagine death as an "endless sleep, unstirred, unillumined by any phantom of dream," [30]—and for him only the unimaginable is impossible. He thought, instead, that perhaps "we may die into a state of dreaming," or that perhaps "life itself . . . will prove to have been in the nature of a dream, and death of an awakening." [31] And, as much of his fiction and poetry suggests, he believed that the dead may communicate with the living.[32] In any case, his sense of humor, proportion, balance—call it what one will—also precluded morbidity in his speculations about life and death. For example, in a characteristically sane and somewhat ironic statement about the matter he conceded that "The whole question of the relation between the living and the dead—who may not remain dead!—is a difficult one." [33] And indeed it is.

[24]

Many readers in this day of scientific exactness may find somewhat exasperating Walter de la Mare's ability to entertain so many speculations without being able to decide upon the ultimate worth of one specific probability. But for many others this ability is one of his most entrancing assets. In a sense one might say he has the ideal Keatsian mind: he was able to rest easily in doubts and uncertainties without any irritable reaching out after fact. Facts were to him of secondary importance. He is not for those who think it is sufficient to know that each human brain contains ten billion or so cells: he was aware of such minutiae—there probably was not one scientific fact discovered or theory advanced in this century of which he did not have knowledge—but he was also aware that facts tell less, and will never tell more, than half of the story of humankind. He was impatient with the scientific-materialistic modern man who, he wrote prophetically in 1935, may someday "parcel out the air, and make a country club of Venus," [34] and he levelled his scorn at the "all but hairless, flesh-eating, pedestrian creature Man" who "has only recently managed to learn to fly, and then insulted heaven and earth with death-laden metal monsters." [35] "It has been left" he wrote also in 1935, "to our own enlightened day to discover the secret of laughing at *everything* that is tainted with the transcendental. . . ." [36]

To the materialists, to the scoffers at anything transcendental, de la Mare has little to say. And should any one be looking for answers, he has none. A characteristic of him is his questioning attitude: "If only questions were as easy to answer as they are to ask!" [37] He questioned everything, never arrogantly, however, because he believed—in fact, it was the only thing he seemed certain of—that all of life is shot with strangeness and mystery;[38] for "we can no more solve the secret of life . . . than that of sleep." [39]

CHAPTER 3

The Short Stories

*A*BANDONED, *lost, missing—hunter, hunted, haunted:* these words best describe the settings, the characters, and the situations of many of Walter de la Mare's short stories. Some of them echo in the mind long after they are read, as do particularly vivid dreams long into the daylight. And some of them are as evanescent, as mysterious. People do not throng in his stories—although he is a master at creating characters—but ghosts may. The very titles of some—"Out of the Deep," "The Riddle," "Missing," "The Revenant," "The Lost Track," "A Recluse," "Strangers and Pilgrims," "What Dreams May Come,"—suggest as much. Yet even the stories whose titles are most prosaic—"Mr. Kempe," "Seaton's Aunt," "Physic," "Crewe," "The Wharf"—are dream and ghost ridden.

Not that de la Mare's tales can be classified in the usual sense as "ghost stories," for there is little in them that is truly remarkable, fantastic, or unbelievable as in "The Monkey's Paw," for example, or other classic ghost stories. De la Mare's settings are firmly anchored in reality, his characters are credible, and the situations in which they find themselves are easily possible. At least, this is so at the beginning of the tales; and, by the time de la Mare ventures into the incredible, the reader has, in Coleridge's phrase, willingly suspended disbelief. He has, in every sense of the word, become enthralled.

I *Point of View*

To achieve, at the onset, a sense of reality and credibility, de la Mare often employs a narrator who tells of an incident in his or someone else's past—a reminiscence. Sometimes he is merely the auditor-recorder of a story told by someone else, a narrator of vivid imagination. In this role, for example, he is the passive soul of rectitude who, in "The Almond Tree," crosses the street in order to avoid the Count and his "disconcerting" companion, whose story he later hears from the Count himself. In this guise, too, he can prepare the reader to be sympathetic to the narrator as happens in "The Bird of Travel," by anticipating, rather unctuously one must admit, the reader's possible objection to the tale: "And at last a quaint old creature whose name I have forgotten . . . told us the following rather pointless story. . . ." As auditor-recorder, he seldom comments except to scoff or to prod the narrator: "Good heavens, Maunders," he interjects at one point in "Lispet, Lispett and Vaine"—and, incidentally, sounds very much like Terence's companion in Housman's poem—"the stuff you talk! But one would not mind so much if you could spin a decent yarn." And his role as auditor-recorder is occasionally so completely subordinated that he disappears entirely before the end of the narrative. Such is the case in "The Creatures," where his sole function is at the outset to lend credibility to the narrator's story.

In many of the first-person tales, however, the recorder device is dropped, and the narrator himself presents a reminiscence of some incident in which he has played a part. The character of the narrator, however, is in many instances similar to that of the auditor-recorder. He is most often unimaginative, dull, stodgy, practical—altogether run-of-the-mill. He is the bumbling, inept Richard in "The Count's Courtship;" he is the boorish Mr. Dash in "A Recluse." The significance of the incident of which he tells, in other words, escapes him; and, because it does, not only does the story remain credible, its irony is intensified.

"Seaton's Aunt" is perhaps one of the best of this kind. Withers, the narrator, is a grown man when he tells this story of one of his schoolmates, Arthur Seaton, a particularly distasteful "foreign" looking boy whose abundance of pocket money, supplied by his mysterious aunt with whom he lives, fails to win any friends among the very British boys of the school. "It needed . . . a rather peculiar taste, a rather rare kind of schoolboy courage and indifference to criticism, to be much associated with him," Withers remembers, and goes on to establish his character by confessing, "And I had neither the taste nor, perhaps, the courage." Seaton, however, bribes Withers with a pot of "outlandish mulberry-coloured jelly" into visiting the home of his aunt over the next holiday.

Upon their arrival at the gloomy Seaton mansion, it is soon obvious to Withers that Arthur is terrified of his aunt—with what seems to be very good reason. "This is the room, Withers, my brother William died in when a boy. Admire the view!" the aunt tells him upon taking him to his room. And, incredibly, Withers does as he is told; his only emotion is dread that the aunt will discover he has brought no luggage! Withers, in other words, is a perfect foil for Arthur Seaton, who is haunted by all manner of mysterious and horrible imaginings which center around his frightening and formidable aunt. "Don't appear to be talking of her, if you wouldn't mind," Arthur pleads, when the boys are alone, adding, "It's—because she's in league with the devil."

To Withers, this is nonsense; and, when in the middle of the night, the terrified Arthur comes to his room with tales of ghosts and evil demons haunting the very house they are in he scoffs: "You may think I'm a jolly noodle; just as you please. . . . Every fellow's a bit off his pluck at night, and you may think it a fine sport to try your rubbish on me." Even later, when Arthur presents to him what would seem to be convincing evidence that something unusual, to say the least, is occurring, Withers says: "I'm going to bed; I've had enough of this foolery."

The second part of the story occurs years later. Arthur Seaton, having left school, has dropped out of Withers' sight—and mind—until one day they meet. Seaton has not changed much; even the fact that he is to be married soon and presumably will be able to leave his aunt's home does not dispell the sense of doom about him. At his invitation, Withers again reluctantly consents to visit, expressly to meet Seaton's fiancée. The atmosphere at the Seaton home is still oppressive, filled with foreboding. Nor has Seaton's aunt changed. Withers again tries to rationalize: "Don't you think perhaps you may not treat your Aunt quite in the right way. . . . I can't help thinking she thinks you don't care for her," he says to his host. But Seaton is inconsolable: "I'm as good as done. You wait," he tells Withers.

Withers does not have long to wait. Several months later he impulsively goes again to the Seaton home to inquire about the newlyweds in a guilty attempt to make amends because he has sent not even a note of congratulation to Seaton upon his marriage which he knew was to have taken place weeks before. But, when he gets to the house, he finds only the aunt; and she refuses to tell him where Seaton and his bride are. As Withers, having been inexplicably left alone, decides to find his way out of the gloomy house, he hears the aunt calling for her nephew: "Arthur, is that you? Is that you, Arthur." When she spies Withers instead, she croaks: "It is you, is it? *That* disgusting man! . . . Go away out. Go away out," which Withers does with alacrity. When he reaches the village he learns that Arthur Seaton has been "dead and buried these three months or more . . . just before he was to be married."

Withers reveals his practical nature when he decides against going to the churchyard to visit Arthur Seaton's grave, for he feels there is "precious little use in pottering about in the muddy dark merely to discover" where the luckless man is buried. But he confesses upon making this decision that he "felt a little uneasy" about it, for "My rather horrible thought was that, so far as I was concerned—one of his extremely few friends—he had never been much better than 'buried' in my mind."

The effect that de la Mare achieves in this and other tales where he uses the stolid, unimaginative narrator is not only realistic but also supremely ironic. We see Seaton only through Withers' work-a-day eyes; the horror Seaton knows is only hinted at; we are left to imagine its enormity; and, unless we supply the pity and the terror, we fail to grasp the larger tragedy that is implied. Yet even in "Seaton's Aunt," in which the suggestion of tragedy is more overt than in many of the other stories, it is easy to miss. The clue is offered in Withers' identification of himself as one of Arthur Seaton's "extremely few friends." Time and again de la Mare's theme concerns the utter loneliness of human beings and their total inability to communicate one with another, a theme of which this story is a good illustration; and the use of the unimaginative narrator or auditor-recorder serves to underline it.

Occasionally—too infrequently, in fact—de la Mare attempted a first-person point of view story which resulted in nothing short of a *tour de force* of realism. "In the Forest," the outstanding example of this type, enters directly into the mind of a small boy; there is no narrator reminiscing, no auditor to provide or imply commentaries on the action. This tale *is* the little boy's; we see the action solely through his eyes—and the horror is that the little boy is so realistic.

The events are simple: the boy's father goes to war; his baby sister sickens and dies; his mother leaves him in the cabin while she takes her dead baby to the village to be buried; the father returns from the battle, mortally wounded; the mother returns. But here is the little boy as he sees these events. He tells of his father's departure: "It was not raining when he [the father] started, only the leaves were wet with rain and the bark of the trees was darkened with wet. I asked him to bring me back a long rifle. He kept rubbing his hands over his face and blinking his eyes and listening to the wind as if he heard the guns. Two or three times he came back to say good-bye to my mother . . . I asked mother if father was glad to be going to the war. But she was crying over the baby, so I went out into the forest till dinner."

Two or three days later he asks his mother how long his father will be at war: "She said she could not tell. And I wondered how they would carry back his body if he was killed in the war." When the baby becomes ill, his mother asks him to go to the village to get the doctor, but he refuses: "It's only crying," he says; and he runs out to go fishing. When he returns, he sees the baby's white face, "and its eyelids were like white wax. Its lips were the colour of its hands, almost blue." He asks if the baby is dead, but his mother does not answer; she "only shook her shoulders." So, the boy continues, "I walked away and looked out of the door."

Left in the cabin alone while his mother has gone to the village to bury the baby, the boy gorges himself from their pitiably small reserve of food, lights a huge fire, and awaits her return. He tells of his reaction to his abandonment: "I could not cry, though I felt very angry at being left alone, and I was afraid." When he awakens the next morning his mother has not yet returned, but he hears a groan outside the door and peeping through a crack recognizes his father: "He was lying on his stomach; his clothes were filthy and torn, and at the back of his shoulder was a small hole pushed in in the cloth. There was dark, thick blood on the withered leaves. I tried to see his face, but couldn't very well. It was all muddy, bleared and white, and he groaned and swore when I touched him. But he didn't know who I was, and some of what he said didn't seem to me to have any sense." As the boy attempts, unsuccessfully, to give his father a drink of water, he tells him about the baby's death; "but he didn't show that he could hear anything; and just as I finished I heard mother coming back from the churchyard." And then comes the last shattering sentence: "So I ran out and told her that it was father."

These extensive quotes from "In the Forest" serve, I hope, to illustrate the exquisite control de la Mare had over point of view and how this control adds to the credibility of his narratives. Not a word is used that is not natural to a young boy; not a sentence is so structured as not to suggest his speech. How controlled and true to the point of view "In the Forest" is can be appreciated when one compares it to another more typical narrative, "The Vats," in which de la Mare uses again the first person. In this story the point of view is no doubt his own. The narrator in this scene is beginning to describe the experience he and a friend had when they came suddenly upon these relics of the past:

In telling of these Vats it is difficult to convey in mere words even a fraction of the effect upon our minds. And not merely our minds. They called to some hidden being within us that, if not their coeval, was at least aware of their exquisite antiquity. Whether of archangelic or daemonic construction, clearly they had remained unvisited by mortal man for as many centuries at least as there are cherries in Damascus or beads in Tierra del Fuego. Sharers of this thought, we two dwarf visitors had whispered an instant or so together, face to face; and then were again mute.

It would be impossible to get farther away in style and tone from "In the Forest."

Yet de la Mare even ventures with some success to see occasionally from a woman's point of view as well, but he most often uses the third person in these instances.

Of those stories from a woman's point of view, "The Wharf" is perhaps the most often commented upon because the central startling image—a dung heap—is so successfully employed to symbolize the beauty and mystery of life.[1] "Cape Race" and " 'A Froward Child,' " however, and "The Face" show de la Mare's mastery of a woman's point of view to even better advantage. In "Cape Race," in which this ability is especially evident, Lettie is a young, romantic girl on her way to America with her betrothed and her future mother-in-law. Filled with life and love, Lettie has just rescued, one early morning on deck, a stray land bird that had lost its way as the ship had passed Cape Race, Newfoundland. Pleased with herself, she impatiently waits for her fiancé who has been seasick for three days. When he finally appears, they go to breakfast in an almost deserted saloon. She wants passionately to kiss him; she has clasped his hand beneath the table. But he sees the waiter bearing down upon them. "Any cereal, Lettie?" he asks, rejecting her gesture of affection. The reader needs no great imagination to guess what their marriage is going to be like.

In " 'A Froward Child' " however, the reader does not have to imagine, for the young woman in this tale breaks off her engagement to much the same kind of man when she discovers how placidly dull her intended husband is. Her agonized question again underscores the theme of loneliness and lack of communication: "Is there nothing in this miserable world can make us realize— *others?*" The same question is implied in "The Face" in which Nora has a transcendental experience, the importance of which she cannot seem to convey to her fiancé. None of these men has the imagination to transcend the mundane world of facts; their inability to do so irrevocably separates them from those to whom they should be closest. Again the theme is estrangement.

Seldom does de la Mare employ the third-person, omniscient point of view; and, in the cases where he does, his tales are either frankly for children, such as some of those in the collection *Broomsticks;* or they are obviously parables or allegories, as are "The Connoisseur" and "The Riddle." In these, no attempt to engage the reader's imagination through an appeal to his sense of reality is made; the stories, often ornately wrought, appeal solely to one's sense of beauty and mystery, and thus are in marked contrast to first-person narratives which create the aura of reality. For, however garrulous de la Mare's narrators are, they are, nevertheless, believable in the same sense that Conrad's Marlow is.

II *Settings*

Another of the ways in which de la Mare creates a sense of reality in his tales is the meticulous accuracy with which he draws his settings. Often, it is true, the action seems to take place in or near a graveyard, as in "Strangers and Pilgrims"; a nearly-deserted decaying mansion, as in "A Recluse"; or an almost abandoned church, as in "All Hallows." Even these somewhat eerie settings, however, are wholly realistic. But few commentators have remarked upon the many settings which are totally unlike these which have somewhat erroneously become exclusively identified as de la Mare trademarks. It is important to examine, therefore, the characteristic de la Mare setting of which the deserted graveyard, mansion, or church are different aspects. For often the action takes place in a mundane setting: the kitchen where Emelia and her small son William share their supper in "Physic"; Mr. Thripp's modest cottage in "The Nap"; the tea shop in "Missing"; the pub in "The Three Friends"; the bedroom and lovely garden in "The Picture"; the doctor's office in "Disillusioned"; a lecture hall in "A Revenant";—and other equally familiar places.

The distinguishing feature about de la Mare's settings is that they are, for the most part, lonely, generally inhabited by only one or two people. They are often rain and windswept, or fog mantled. Seldom does anything occur in bright sunshine; the time in most of the stories is usually twilight or after dark.

Even during the daylight, if events occur, say, in a garden, as they do in "Miss Duveen," they take place in a shaded part of the garden: "It was raining," the narrator of "Miss Duveen" remembers of his first meeting with that delightful and pitiable creature for whom his story is titled: "the raindrops falling softly into the unrippled water, making their great circles, and tapping on the motionless leaves above my head where I sat in shelter on the bank. But the sun was shining whitely from behind a thin fleece of cloud, when Miss Duveen suddenly peeped in at me out of the greenery. . . ." In another typical setting, Dr. Lidgett's consulting room in "Disillusioned," as the doctor talks to the stranger who has confronted him, "It was afternoon, and a scene of stillest life. The polished writing table . . . the cabinet . . . the glass and gilt of the engraved portraits on the walls—everything in the room appeared to have sunken long ago into a reverie oceans deep."

Even when one would normally expect to find numbers of people—as, for example, in "What Dreams May Come" where the action seems to take place on a bus—we find the central character "*alone* now in the strange vacancy of the coach. . . ." It has been raining, "raining heavily . . . the dark stain on the thick grey fabric of the seat had soaked it through." She looks about for the conductor, but "The wreathing mist which dimmed her eyes obscured him too a little. . . ." Similarly, de la Mare draws his setting for "The Three Friends," two of whom are approaching a pub as the story begins: "The street was narrow; yet, looking up, the two old friends, bent on their accustomed visit, could discern— beyond a yellow light that had suddenly shone out into the hushed gloom from an attic window—the vast, accumulated thunderclouds that towered into the darkening zenith."

And the pub's interior, where the two friends discuss with the barmaid one's reoccurring dream of death, is no more cheerful an atmosphere. In much the same way, railway carriages and stations, contrary to one's usual expectation—and experience—never seem to be occupied by more than two people; and, as the trains travel through the dark from nowhere to nowhere, a story unfolds, as in "The Creatures," which takes the reader just as effortlessly into what de la Mare calls the "otherwhere." Trains, coaches, carriages of one sort or another often figure, in fact, in these tales; and they serve to underline de la Mare's belief that we are all travelers whose points of departure and destinations are, for the most part, forever unknown.

Besides the pervasive sense of loneliness achieved by the location of the action, the limited number of characters, the weather and time of day, there are other aspects of his settings which amount almost to de la Mare signatures: windows and mirrors—which often serve the same function—and portraits. In nearly every one of de la Mare's stories mirrors and windows play some part. In "Physic," for example, William, the little boy who becomes suddenly ill, begs his mother to put down the blinds to the very bottom of the window because, he says, "I *hate* seeing—seeing myself in the glass." And later he asks his mother, "Why do faces come in the window, horrid faces?" In "The Talisman," the narrator catches a glimpse of himself in a mirror and also sees "another reflection, a phantom face. . . ." In "What Dreams May Come," Emmeline, apparently dozing in a bus, wakes knowing she has been looking at a reflection other than her own in the window. For the little girl in "Selina's Parable," "every window . . . had a charm, an incantation all its own." And the reason given in the story for this charm might well have been de la Mare's own: "Was it not an egress for her eye to a scene of some beauty, or life, or of forbiddingness; was it not the way of light; either her own outward, or the world's inward?"

Windows and mirrors, even when only mentioned in the stories, take on a symbolic—one would almost like to say "mystic"—force. We know that de la Mare was fascinated by them, for he felt that through them and in them one can see the other side of things or of the self. For the same reason, incidentally, the feature of his characters' faces most often mentioned is their eyes; they were to him, in a Blakean sense, windows of the soul: "There is at times a dweller behind the eye that looks out, though only now and again, from that small window," observes the narrator of "The Green Room." This idea occurs again and again throughout the tales.

Perhaps one of the best illustrations of how de la Mare combines these symbols is to be found in "The Picnic," in the collection *On The Edge* (1930). In this tale, Miss Curtis, a seemingly very practical, feet-on-the-ground London shopkeeper, recalls a sea-side vacation she took five years earlier. During the course of her holiday she sees daily a man at a window who appears always to smile when she passes. His smile is a "quiet" one, "far away," and, she decides, "lonely." It seems to her to plead for her love, her understanding. And, of course, she falls in love with him. The last day of her vacation she sees him out walking with a companion; they confront one another; and she looks up "straight into the unknown one's face, straight into his eyes." But, although they look straight at her, they do not see her—and have never seen her. The stranger is blind. Miss Curtis, as the story concludes, shuts up her shop for the evening, her last act being to pull down "the last dark-blue blind, the blind that covered the glass of the door." This action is symbolic of her renunciation of five years before when she had embarked not on a love affair, but a "life affair"; for "this life of which she had caught this marvellous glimpse had itself never even been a possibility—merely an illusion."

In much the same manner as the windows and mirrors, portraits play a role and have a symbolic function in the short stories. In "Seaton's Aunt" for example, in a superb combination of two symbols, there is a hideous water color hanging in Withers' room of an enormous eye "with an extremely fishlike intensity in the spark of light on the dark pupil"; beneath it is inscribed "Thou God Seest ME." In "What Dreams May Come" the portrait of the master of the house in which Emmeline finds herself is in reality a death's head. In yet another tale, "The Picture," Lucia is haunted by the painting of the dead first wife of her adored husband. And, in the masterful depiction of hatred called "An Anniversary," a portrait "appears as if what it represented were always steadily in wait for . . . a renewed and really close scrutiny of itself." De la Mare observes in this story, and illustrates the idea often, that portraits can "shed on one a sort of passive influence."

The influence of Walter Beverley's dead aunt's portrait in "The Quincunx" is, however, something other than passive. In this story, which again treats of hatred, Walter becomes obsessed by his aunt's portrait and finally is possessed by her malignant influence. But, in this case, he is so churlish and rapacious that the reader's sympathy is, however grudgingly given, with the dead aunt.

The most finely wrought story in which most of these symbols— windows, mirrors, and portraits—appear is "The Looking Glass," which echoes Lewis Carroll only in the title and in the name of the central character; for the Alice of this tale goes through the looking glass in a far different manner than Carroll's Alice does. The consumptive young companion of an old shrew, de la Mare's Alice wanders daily during her free time in the walled-in garden in which raindrops always seem to be quietly falling. She knows the garden is haunted at times and feels the presence of its ghost: "What was all through the place now like smoke Alice perceived to be the peculiar clarity of the air discernible in the garden at times. The clearness as it were of glass, of a looking-glass, which conceals all behind and beyond it, returning only the looker's wonder, or simply her vanity, or even her gaiety." And Alice smiles to think that "There are people who look into looking-glasses, actually see themselves there, and yet never turn a hair."

The garden is the only place where Alice feels at peace with herself. She tells her confidant, Sarah, the cook next door: "I get out of bed at night to look down from the window and wish myself here. When I'm reading, just as if it were a painted illustration —in the book, you know—the scene of it all floats in between me and the print." Having been told by Sarah that she may accost the presence in the garden by following a certain ritual, Alice prepares to do so—even more eagerly when she discovers that she is herself, in a sense, the presence. "The spirit is *me*," she is convinced: "*I* haunt this place."

On the night of her assignation with that spirit she gazes at herself in the "dim discoloured glass" in her own room. Why her mirror is so described is all too apparent; for, when her employer tries to awaken her the next morning, Alice, "though unbeknown in any really conscious sense to herself, perhaps, had long since decided not to be awakened." She has, in other words, gone through to the other side of the looking glass and clarity of the garden to the real reality, an experience similar to Nora's in "The Face" who felt, when she fell into a woodland pond whose glassy surface had enchanted her, that she "had gone in under a dark dreadful tunnel and come out on the other side."

Water, as can be seen from this discussion, also plays an important symbolic function in the short stories; but, because it has an even more important role in the novels, its function has been analyzed extensively in the section devoted to them. Suffice it to say here, water—whether in the form of rain, or a stream, or a pool, or the sea—is used occasionally as an estranging medium, as is the stream in "Miss Duveen" or in "The Lost Track." Sometimes it represents the source of reality, as the sea does in "The Picnic," or the still pool in "The Face." Most often, as rain it serves not only to increase the sense of isolation but also to suggest life-giving (or truth-giving, for de la Mare) properties traditionally associated with rain.[2]

In the stories of Walter de la Mare, then, the settings have a two-fold function: they provide a realistic background on which the sometimes bizarre action is projected, and they serve to increase the significance of the action by assuming a symbolic role. That de la Mare learned much from Emily Bronte, Thomas Hardy, W. H. Hudson and Joseph Conrad about these matters he himself was happy to admit; and that he learned his lessons well is obvious from the stories themselves. But no story, however perfect its setting, is successful for this reason alone—characters and themes must be at least as felicitous.

III *Characterization*

Edward Wagenknecht and other critics have pointed to the brief but incisive strokes with which de la Mare created his characters.[3] But to an even greater extent, his mastery is due to the fact that generally he does not describe his characters—they reveal themselves by their actions and their speech. We have already seen Seaton's baleful aunt welcome his young friend: "This is the room, Withers, my brother William died in when a boy. Admire the view." The juxtaposition of the comment and the command tell more of Seaton's aunt than would have pages of description. In much the same way, the malignant butler in "Crewe," after having goaded the gardener to his death, says of him, "And yet—why, he never so much as asked me to say a good word for him. Not one," thus revealing his hypocrisy, and his true nature. So too, Aubrey, the jealous husband in "An Anniversary," reveals himself when, railing at his wife, he refers to Othello as "that pimp of futility," and thus unconsciously applies the epithet to himself. Even the thoroughly delightful and completely mad Miss Miller in the story of that name shows just how mad and how delightful she is when she first opens her mouth to talk to the runaway Nella; and her story of herself as a young child, when things ran away from her rather than her running away from them, reminds us that, as Emily Dickinson wrote, in "much madness is divinest sense to a discerning eye."

In fact, although few of his characters are as engagingly demented as Miss Miller is (although Miss Rawlings, in "Pigtails, Ltd." runs a close second to her), a good many of them are mad, at least in the sense of being possessed or obsessed or, as occurs in several of the tales—haunted. A good example of one who is obsessed—in this case by the idea of pure beauty, as is Anthony in "Lispet, Lispett and Vaine"—is the artist in "The Tree." He is effectively contrasted to his half brother, a fruit merchant, who also is obsessed, but by money and the desire to "get ahead." The narrator of "The Creatures" is another character obsessed by a vision he has seen of paradise; and the recluse in "Mr. Kempe" searches with unremitting ardor for proof of man's possession of a soul, a search similar to that carried on by the central character in "A Recluse." Then too, there is the young man in "Pretty Poll" who fell in love with one of the imagined former owners—the "impossible she"—of a parrot he had purchased which alternately swore like a sailor and sang like an angel.

In many of the tales the obsession of the central character amounts to his being haunted. In these tales there is a feeling of tension, an undertone of mystery and strangeness that not only fascinates but terrifies the reader. They sometimes resemble the auditor-recorder's description of the narrator's tale in "Bird of Travel": "a poet's story in sober earnest: incoherent, obscure, unreal, unlifelike, without an ending." But they have these qualities only if one looks at them straight on, so to speak; for—just as life itself is sometimes incoherent, obscure, unreal, and, indeed, "unlifelike"—so are the stories. "Qui vive?"—"who goes there?"—the question de la Mare most often asks, is often answered in the tales by another question: "Who asks?" And because he felt that "fiction holds up, or should hold up, an all-searching, all-collective, and reflective mirror to humanity . . ." [4] his stories hold the mirror to that part of humanity seldom touched upon except in "shockers" or in science fiction.

Most of de la Mare's haunted characters are also solitaries, perhaps because he felt that each of us is, in a sense, a "livelong [*sic.*] recluse," did we have the courage to admit it.[5] But, more likely, his characters are solitaries in these particular stories because his experience had taught him that "strange and uninvited guests are likely to intrude on any protracted human solitude. . . ." [6] That there may be ghosts, revenants—call them what one will—seemed completely plausible to him: time and again he speculated in his essays on the possibility, and the theme of many of his stories concerns just this eventuality. Against any charge that such stories are not "realistic," he would have replied what he wrote in another connection: "What is called realism is usually a record of life at a low pitch and ebb viewed in the sunless light of day. . . ." [7]

As I have said earlier in this chapter, most of these stories are realistic enough, in the beginning at least; and, by the time they have begun to engage "the little nowhere" of the reader's mind, the purpose of the early "realism" has been accomplished and the magic begins to work. I have already referred to "Seaton's Aunt" in this connection, but I think in many ways the aunt in the first-person narrative called "The Guardian," which appears in *A Beginning* (1955), is even more diabolical because she does not comprehend at all what occurs to her and her nephew Philip, who becomes haunted not only by evil and ugliness but by good and beauty as well.

We listen to her as she describes herself: "I am not a mother. I am what is called 'an old maid'; but even 'old maids,' I assume, are entitled to their convictions." And we savor the magnificent irony when, just after she describes her young nephew as a "delicate . . . sensitive and solitary child" whom she loves dearly, she goes on to describe herself as a child: "I dreaded company . . . was shy of speaking my own mind, and of showing affection. I used both to despise and to envy the delicate—the demonstrative. . . ." As the story progresses, it becomes obvious that she has not changed. She advises Philip's mother against sending the boy to school until his ninth year, at which time, she says, "I had the pleasure and privilege of paying for Philip's education." He is bundled off to a preparatory school "where even a sensitive and difficult child might have at least every opportunity of doing well and of being happy." Of this she is certain, because, as she says, "I had myself insisted on being taken over the whole school, scullery to attics, and on having a few words *alone* with the matron. . . ." She soon finds that Philip is prey to some kind of "nervous trouble" when on a holiday from school he confesses to her that he sees something that is not in the room but "inside"—presumably, "inside" his head. The very soul of practicality and insensitiveness, she continues: "By dint of careful questioning, I discovered at length that what troubled him was no more, as I thought at the time, than a mere fancy."

Put on a regimen of tonic, Philip appears to recover from his nervous trouble and his aunt is relieved; for, as she knows, "Even people of excellent common sense may occasionally be the prey of illusions—ghosts and similar nonsense. Charles Wesley, for example." However, a few weeks after his twelfth birthday, Philip falls one night from the window ledge of his school dormitory, and his aunt is summoned to his deathbed. Seated beside the dying boy, she confesses: "At that time I had already steeled myself to many things in this world; but a life, I can truthfully declare, was slipping away far from me more precious than my own . . . I had never, except once before, felt helpless and forsaken." At this moment the dormitory maid—whose face vaguely recalls to the aunt "some old picture I had seen"—comes into the room and over the dying boy's face appears a look "as near human ecstasy as mortal features are capable of." And, although the aunt detests "anything even resembling sentimentality," she recognizes that Philip is in love—"the poor child," she calls him, "was in love." The evil presence that had haunted him has been overcome by this love; and, though he dies, he has achieved more happiness than the aunt will ever know.

Philip and Arthur Seaton are just two of several haunted boys or young men in de la Mare's tales: there is Jimmie, in the less-successful "Out of the Deep," who returns to the hated house in which he had grown up, having been willed it by his equally detested late aunt and uncle. As a boy, he had slept in the attic; upon his return, he sleeps in his Uncle Timothy's Arabian bed by which hangs a bell cord and around which he burns every night all night candles because as a child he had been so terrified of the dark. He recalls too from his youth the hated butler Soames; and one evening, having sampled too much of the contents of his uncle's wine cellar, he pulls the bell cord. A spectral Soames answers. Jimmie jocularly asks for primroses; and, although it is the dead of winter, almost instantaneously a lovely young child enters the room with a bowl of them. Each successive pull of the bell cord summons something "out of the deep," and at last the haunted Jimmie goes mad and is found dead in his old bed in the attic.

De la Mare does well in getting into the mind of a madman, as Jimmie in "Out of the Deep" obviously is; and he does equally well with a young man who is haunted by the face of a lovely, unknown suicide in "The Green Room" and with the old man in "The House," every room of which is filled with ghosts. Sometimes, however, his stories have as their central characters revenants themselves. Such a one is "Strangers and Pilgrims," a story so filled with pathos as to linger—like an unhappy ghost itself—long in the reader's mind. Such also is "A Revenant"—about the shade of Edgar Allan Poe who stops in to hear a lecture about himself given by Professor Monk who purports to be objective and bal-

anced in his treatment but who in reality damns Poe—and himself
—with his preference for "facts" to "atmosphere." This story, however, is more interesting to the student of literature as a discussion
of how not to approach the works of an author than it is as a story
about de la Mare's preoccupation with the possibilities of the
dead returning.

But there are many other kinds of characters in de la Mare's
short stories than the obsessed, the mad, and the haunted; and,
although the theme of the returning dead is a central one, there
are others as well. True, de la Mare seldom bothers with the "average person"; but, as he enquired in his own person elsewhere,
"Where shall we find an average *mind* or personality or soul or
self?" [8] About as close as he ever comes to it is in "The Nap" in
which we see bared the thoughts about his wife and children of a
lower middle-class man, Mr. Thripp. This story illustrates also another of de la Mare's preoccupations which I have already touched
upon: the difficulty, if not altogether the impossibility, of communication or understanding between people. This theme is central
or is touched upon in many of the tales.

Usually the inability to communicate is the result of a lack of
imagination or love on the part of one of the characters. I have
already mentioned " 'A Froward Child' " and "Cape Race" as good
examples of this situation, but many other stories, such as "The
Count's Courtship," "The Tree," "Disillusioned," and "The Face,"
are in whole or in part about the inability of human beings to
establish some kind of communication with others. Even Miss
Duveen, in the story of the same name, is unable to maintain
more than briefly the interest of the little boy who tells years later
the story of this mad—and pitiful—old lady. Enchanted at first by
her, he confesses when she is "put away" that, despite "a vague
sorrow" he feels when he hears the news, he is "greatly relieved."
No more pathetic a scene in all of de la Mare is there than the one
when Miss Duveen, before her departure, throws a letter to him
from across the stream which separates their two gardens: "She
whispered earnestly and rapidly at me over the water. But I could
not catch a single word she said, and failed to decipher her close
spidery handwriting." Even after this they see each other occasionally across the stream, but the narrator recalls: "The distance

seemed to confuse her, and quite silenced me." The distance across the stream, of course, is as immeasurable and vast as the distances in the unplumbable sea that separates, as it did for Matthew Arnold, island from island forever.

In another vein entirely are the stories in *Broomsticks and Other Tales* (1925), tales de la Mare had written for his own children and which, I am sure, will continue to delight children as long as there are any to read or be read to. The basic themes are to be found even in these, however: the haunted, the dead returning, estrangement. Characteristically, these are no run-of-the-mill children's stories—they rank easily with Kenneth Grahame's *Wind in the Willows*, A. A. Milne's Pooh stories, or Lewis Carroll's Alice tales. In fact, de la Mare excels other writers for children, I believe, simply because—and I almost hate to use the word again—his characters are more *real*. True, there is fantasy as when, for example, the jealous father of the lovely Myfanwy turns into an ass; but it is perfectly logical that he do so, because he eats a magic apple which turns anyone who does so into exactly what he really is. And, of course, it hardly seems likely that Alice's godmother is really her great-great-great-great-great-great-great-great grandmother; but how else can she be three hundred and fifty years old? Such is de la Mare's artistry that these and similar fancies become entirely possible.

Although, of course, the ultimate judges of children's stories must be children themselves, none of the tales in *Broomsticks* can be read by an adult without some delight and profit for some of them illustrate his profoundest insights. Such, for example, is the story of the thief who craved of all things happiness but does not find it until he marries Susan—the one servant who refuses to leave him because, as she says to him, "You was less unkind to me than to all the other servants put together,"—and then gives away all of his ill-gotten gains. What redeems him is seeing Susan with a look of happiness on her face and realizing that, although he had never seen a "lovelier sight," neither he nor any other thief could steal it.

Perhaps the most engaging of the stories in *Broomsticks*, and the most deceptively simple, is "Maria-Fly." Although it can be read as a story about the inability of human beings to communicate with each other, it is, without doubt, based on William Blake's poem "The Fly"; the key stanza and the primary theme of "Maria-Fly" is stated in the poem's second stanza:

> Am not I
> A fly like thee?
> Or art not thou
> A man like me?

The story also illustrates one of de la Mare's abiding beliefs, the clearest example of which is in the introduction to *Behold, This Dreamer!*—"All things stale and lose their virtue, the best and worst, the simple and complicated, the plain and beautiful, impulse as well as artifice, *unless we attend to them;* give to them as much at least as they can bestow."

The little girl, Maria, in the story does just that: for the first time in her whole life she *sees* a fly. And, watching the fly with the closest attention, "It seemed to be that just as Maria herself was one particular little girl, so this was one particular fly. A fly by itself. A fly living its own one life; confident, alert, alone in its own Fly World." Soon, she becomes engrossed, and then the strangest thing happens: "She seemed almost to have *become* the fly—Maria-Fly." After this experience, although she could not have explained why, "she felt surprisingly gay and joyful." But no one who remembers the joy of childhood "watching" a burdened ant toil up the seemingly insurmountable Everest of a blade of grass needs to be told why Maria is so happy. De la Mare caught the rapture perfectly, and also captured the poignancy of the aftermath of Maria's experience: she wants to tell someone about what really happened, what it was like to really see a fly. And, of course, as even the most poetic of mystics fails to communicate the truth of his experience of God, so is Maria unable to tell anyone the truth of her experience.

She tries in turn to tell the cook, a visiting clergyman, the seamstress, her father, the gardener, and finally his simple-minded helper. But even he does not understand. She turns away from him "her small head filled as with a tune ages old and as sorrowful as the sounds of the tide on the unvisited shores of the ocean," and goes to sit alone in an arbor. After some moments in which we do not know her thoughts, the story ends: "Maria gave yet another deep sigh, and then looked up around her almost as if in hopes of somebody else to whom she might tell her secret tale—about the fly—about Maria-Fly. And then, as if at a signal, she hopped down suddenly out of the arbour, almost as lightly as a thin-legged bird herself, and was off flying over the emerald green grass into the delightful sunshine without in the least knowing why, or where to." Perhaps Maria has learned what the speaker in Blake's poem knows:

> Then am I
> A happy fly,
> If I live
> Or if I die.

As de la Mare does in the rest of his fiction, he shows in his stories for children his profound knowledge of and love for all things living. But the children's stories allow him to show also, as he seldom can in his other fiction, his delightful sense of humor and love of nonsense. There is, for example, Sam Such, who grows into manhood thinking his nose is made of wax. His father, "a prosperous clothier and haberdasher," has a shop named "Such & Such"; and the store's motto is "Why go to So and So's when you can get ALL you will ever want from Such & Such." And there is Miss Chauncey of "Broomsticks" who is deceived by her cat—but then there are a hundred more touches of humor which cannot be really enjoyed unless the stories *and* the poems *and* the novels are read.

But one does not read de la Mare for his humor, however delightful it may be. One goes to him to see in tangible form the truths, the dreams and longings—and forebodings and terrors—known alone by and admitted only to the inmost self. This is not to say that all of the tales are equally satisfactory or successful. Some of them are contrived, a bit too pat—"Out of the Deep," "The Green Room," and "A Revenant" come immediately to mind. But even these have their interest, and it is only fair that he be judged as are Wordsworth and Keats and even Shakespeare—by his best. His best stories are superb. "Miss Duveen," "In the Forest," "The Looking Glass," "Seaton's Aunt," "Miss Miller," "The

Bowl," "Pigtails, Ltd.," "Lucy," "Missing," "Neighbours," "The Orgy: An Idyll," "An Ideal Craftsman," "The Nap," "The Wharf," and "The Trumpet" are among the best short stories written.

His preoccupation with good and evil puts him on a level with Hawthorne and Conrad; his mastery of suspense and terror is equal to Poe's; the subtlety of his characterizations occasionally rivals James'. And the range of his portrayals is impressive: children, old maids, the demented, old idealists and young pessimists, artists, businessmen, dandys, young women in love—all of whom share in the mysterious and sometimes maddening business called living.

CHAPTER 4

The Poetry

SINCE the publication in 1902 of *Songs of Childhood* under the pseudonym of Walter Ramal, de la Mare's reputation has rested principally on his poetry. What anthology of recent British poetry has not included "The Listeners"? What school child has not, at one time or another, intoned " 'Is there anybody there?' said the Traveller . . ." and has not wondered who, really, is the Traveller? Happily, some have gone on to read more of de la Mare's poetry to find that, in the poet's view, we are all Travellers and all Listeners.

So often, however, have the words "childlike" and "faerie" been applied to de la Mare's poetry that all but the most careful readers are likely to think of the poet as having a rather fey and delightful, but a little too precious, imagination; that his poetry is not about the real world at all. Nothing, of course, can be further from the truth. For de la Mare was aware that in the very innocence of childhood can be found the later evil:

> The shadow of a poplar tree
>   Lay in that lake of sun,
> As I with my little sword went in—
>   Against a thousand, one.
>
> Haughty and infinitely armed,
>   Insolent in their wrath,
> Plumed high with purple plumes they held
>   The narrow meadow path.
>
> The air was sultry; all was still;
>   The sun like flashing glass;
> And snip-snap my light-whispering steel
>   In arcs of light did pass.

Lightly and dull fell each proud head,
  Spiked keen without avail,
Till swam my uncontented blade
  With ichor green and pale

. . . .

The very air trembled in fear;
  Eclipsing shadow seemed
Rising in crimson waves of gloom—
  On one who dreamed.

This poem, "The Massacre," published in 1906, is about a child, yes, but it is also about evil. And, in one of the last volumes of poems de la Mare was to publish, *The Burning Glass* (1945), we see in "Laid Low" and old man ill abed:

Nought else now stirring my sick thoughts to share,
Laid low, I watched the house-flies in the air;
Swarthy, obscene, they angled, gendering there.
And Death, who every daybreak now rode by—

. . . .

Jerked in his saddle, and laughed into the sky . . .

. . . .

                    My heart said,
"Nay, there is nought to fear"—yet shook with dread:
Wept, "Call him back!": groaned, "Ah! that eyeless head!"

Impassioned by its beauty; sick with doubt:—
"Oh God, give life!" and, "Would that I were dead!"

Nothing could be more real, less faerie and childlike, than these two poems from his early and late career. But to try to swing the pendulum too far in the other direction, to claim that de la Mare's poetry is realistic in the accepted sense of the word would be to do a disservice to a poet who, I think, may well rank in time to come, at least in certain respects, with Yeats. There is, of course, no place here to go into a detailed comparison of the two poets; but Yeats, although unquestionably the greater poet, appeals to-day to a certain extent because of his complexity. As T. S. Eliot and a score of others have reminded us, modern poetry is complex because the age is complex. But perhaps in this idea lies the explanation for de la Mare's apparent simplicity: he is not reflecting this age or any other specific time. He is not topical—a word which, paradoxically, can be applied to Yeats; he is not Romantic, Victorian, Georgian; he is not even metaphysical although W. H. Auden suggests that in his later work there are suggestions of metaphysical wit.[1] De la Mare's finest poetry—and a great deal of it is fine—is above, or beyond, topicality.

Perhaps the real difficulty in the term "childlike" is that it connotes "childish" to a great many people who probably also confuse sentiment with sentimentality. If one agrees with de la Mare's conception that the "childlike" imagination is opposed to that of "boyhood" (discussed fully in my chapter on the imagination), one must agree that de la Mare's own imagination is childlike; that is to say, it is "intuitive, inductive" rather than "logical, deductive." It is true, also, that de la Mare wrote a good many poems about and for children: a rough estimate of the number of poems in his collection of children's poems, *Rhymes and Verses* (1947) shows approximately six hundred poems. But they are not by any means poems exclusively for children; and, if one thinks of children as having the sensibilities that the "Run, Dick, Run," authors seem to think they have, these poems are not for children at all. For example, one may cite "The Fly":

> How large unto the tiny fly
>   Must little things appear!—
> A rosebud like a feather bed,
>   Its prickle like a spear;
>
> A dewdrop like a looking-glass,
>   A hair like golden wire;
> The smallest grain of mustard-seed
>   As fierce as coals of fire;
>
> A loaf of bread, a lofty hill;
>   A wasp, a cruel leopard;
> And specks of salt as bright to see
>   As lambkins to a shepherd.

Or, for another example, "At the Keyhole":

> "Grill me some bones," said the Cobbler,
>   "Some bones, my pretty Sue;

I'm tired of my lonesome with heels and soles,
Springsides and uppers too;
A mouse in the wainscot is nibbling;
A wind in the keyhole drones;
And a sheet webbed over my candle, Susie,—
    Grill me some bones!"

"Grill me some bones," said the Cobbler,
    "I sat at my tic-tac-to;
And a footstep came to my door and stopped,
And a hand groped to and fro;
And I peered up over my boot and last;
And my feet went cold as stones:—
I saw an eye at the keyhole, Susie!—
    Grill me some bones!"

These poems (and hundreds of others could have been cited) show that what is childlike in de la Mare is that same awareness and perception that one finds in William Blake and Emily Dickinson, both of whom he resembles more than superficially.[2] They also illustrate my feeling that de la Mare's poems are not topical: they do not reflect this age any more than they do any other historical period. As W. H. Auden recently pointed out, in de la Mare's poetry there are no machines and no modern buildings.[3] One could easily go further: there is no concern with politics or history, or with creeds or with religion itself; neither is he a philosopher, for he has no specific answers to the epistemological and teleological questions all philosophers must somehow answer.

I Themes

If these are none of Walter de la Mare's concerns, then what is his poetry about? It is about nothing more or less than the human condition. *Who are we? What are we? Whence? Whither? Why?* —these are the major themes not only of his poetry but also of his fiction. To define these questions, let alone to attempt to answer them, is to make even the most inarticulate among us, in a sense, poets. Adequately to define them is what de la Mare did. He did not, however, propose any answers: there is no progression (or retreat, some might call it), as in Eliot's poetry; there is no reaching for certainties, as in Yeats's. In a sense, de la Mare is more nearly like Aldous Huxley, who continued to grope intellectually although he seemed certain that there were no answers. De la Mare continued to explore, but his was an emotional, intuitive search and therefore more sure. In other words, although Huxley mistrusted intellectualism, he was unable to escape from it and thus became disillusioned; de la Mare, although he too mistrusted the intellect, still was able to retain the belief that life is somehow meaningful. He knew he did not know the answers; he knew he could never know them; but he did not despair. Nor did he think life is a cosmic joke because he knew that someone or something would have had to have played it, and his poetry shows he was uncertain even about the existence of a someone or something:

> Starven with cares, like tares in wheat,
> Wildered with knowledge, chilled with doubt,
> The timeless self in vain must beat
> Against its walls to hasten out
> Whither the living waters fount . . .
> (from "Dreams," *The Fleeting* [1933])

It is the "timeless self," then, about which de la Mare was concerned. But notice, this "self" *must* beat against its walls *in vain.* This conception, central in all of his work, removes him forever from any consideration as "childlike" or "faerie" in the usual senses of those terms. This conception also explains his preoccupation with death, dreams, the supernatural, children, and nature. These divisions are artificial, for all of his poetry is of a piece; nevertheless, for purposes of discussion, they are convenient.

II *Death*

Death is one of de la Mare's preoccupations, but the fascination is by no means a morbid one. His attitude is ambiguous; he is, as is the old man in "Laid Low," "Impassioned by its beauty; sick with doubt." Significantly, the note is struck in the first poem in the volume of 1906:

> The loveliest thing earth hath, a shadow hath,
> A dark and livelong hint of death,
> Haunting it ever till its last faint breath.
>   Who, then, may tell
> The beauty of heaven's shadowless asphodel?

And the shadow continues to fall, decreasingly nostalgic, increasingly ironic until the last volume; as in these lines from "De Profundis" published in *O, Lovely England* (1953). Speaking of that last habitation, the grave, he says:

> You will not be cold there;
> You will not wish to see your face in a mirror;
> There will be no heaviness,
> Since you will not be able to lift a finger.
>
> . . . .
>
> There will be no recognition;
> No one, who should see you, will say—
> Throughout the uncountable hours—

"Why . . . the last time we met, I brought you some flowers!"

Nostalgia is a prominent emotion in many of the poems, for the archetypal fall from grace, or expulsion from paradise, is a major element in his poems about death. Man is an exile who has come "By some dark catastrophe/ Far, far from home" ("Astray"). He is a stranger on earth "whose every exiled day" aches with the memory of the lost Eden ("Exile"). He is "that Adam who, with Snake for guest,/ Hid anguished eyes upon Eve's piteous breast"; who wonders whether, "from wide circuit, shall at length I see/ Pure daybreak lighten again on Eden's tree?" ("Exile").

Death, then, is possibly the means by which one returns home; and this is why it lures and fascinates de la Mare. In death one may win to that place "Where blooms the flower when her petals fade/ . . . Where all things transient to the changeless win" ("Vain Questioning"). Thus, he sometimes longs for death: "Heavenly Archer, bend thy bow/ Now the flame of life burns low,/Youth is gone; I, too, would go" ("Dust to Dust"). Countless poems reflect this longing: he cries, "O ardent dust,/ Turn to thy grave,/ And quiet have!" ("Reconciliation"). Nevertheless, one cannot be sure that death will bring one home. "Think not because I am silent, I forget," warns the voice from the grave in "The Taciturn." And the Self speaking to Self wonders,

> If thou wake never—well:
> But if perchance thou find

> Light, that brief gloom behind,
> Thou'lt have wherewith to tell
> If thou'rt in heaven or hell! ("Self to Self")

Yet another indication that death may not bring the exile home is seen in a sonnet published in *Poems* (1906): Death tells the speaker, "Even in the grave thou wilt have thyself." Of one thing only can we be sure: death will come—

> Walk in beauty. Vaunt thy rose.
> Flaunt thy transient loveliness.
> Pace for pace with thee there goes
> A shape that hath not come to bless.
> ("The Quiet Enemy")

Man is "a transient object in this vast" who

> Sighs o'er a universe transcending thought,
> Afflicted by vague bodings of the past,
> Driven toward a future, unforseen, unsought,

and seeks "Companion in earth's dwelling-place" ("The Flower").
Only seldom does de la Mare introduce, as he does in "The Flower," the idea of God. Nor as Charles Williams, Graham Greene, and others have pointed out, does he subscribe at all to orthodox or traditional Christianity.[1] In "The Flower," for example, man seeks a "Companion." A similar idea is expressed in the significantly titled "Vacant Day," in which the speaker is seen

> Longing in vain for him to come
> Who had breathed such blessedness
>
> On this fair world, wherein we pass
> So chequered and so brief a stay;
> And yearned in spirit to learn, alas,
> What kept him still away.

De la Mare had asked in an even earlier poem "The Miracle" (1906)

Who beckons the green ivy up
  Its solitary tower of stone?
What spirit lures the bindweed's cup
    Unfaltering on?
Calls even the starry lichen to climb
By agelong inches endless Time?

—and had found no answer. The concluding two stanzas clearly indicate the vanity of even hoping for a positive answer:

So creeps ambition on; so climb
  Man's vaunting thoughts. He, set on high,
Forgets his birth, small space, brief time,
    That he shall die;
Dreams blindly in his stagnant air;
Consumes his strength; strips himself bare;

Rejects delight, ease, pleasure, hope,
  Seeking in vain, but seeking yet,
Past earthly promise, earthly scope,
    On one aim set:
As if, like Chaucer's child, he thought
All but "O Alma!" nought.

Even late in life de la Mare gives no indication in his poetry of a positive belief in the existence of God. That this is so is revealed in "The Traveller" (1945), the last poem of any significance he was to write. This poem is characteristically titled; but, as Victoria Sackville-West suggested in her Wharton Lecture on de la Mare, one should take care not to read into the poem "a very obvious and platitudinous set of philosophical ideas." However, although she accurately states that to de la Mare "the whole of life is a journey; he is acutely aware of our pilgrimage towards some mysterious bourne; he is, himself, the constant traveller," [5] she reads the poem inaccurately, perhaps even platitudinously. She finds in the poem an "affirmation of faith" because the Traveller prays "to a mysterious, but, in the last resort, a pitiful God," and she compares the Traveller to Coleridge's Ancient Mariner.

  Far closer, however, is the poem in spirit to Browning's "Childe Roland," for the Traveller is one of those who

> had faced life's long duress,
> Its pangs and horrors, anguish, hardship, woes,
> Their one incentive ever on to press,
>
> Defying dread and danger—and in vain:
> Not to achieve a merely temporal goal,
> Not for bright glory, praise, or greed of gain,
> But in that secret craving of the soul
>
> For what no name has; flow'r or hidden stem. . . .

This Traveller's journey is over the "very *Eye of Earth*" (de la Mare's italics) which is very much like the wasteland that has figured prominently in poetry since Browning. Reaching its center, the Traveller is moved impulsively to pour "hoarsely forth a babble of praise and prayer." There is "no living soul to hear or heed him there"; but—and this is crucial—de la Mare continues:

> A self there is that listens in the heart
> To what is past the range of human speech,
> Which yet 'twould seem, has tidings to impart—
> The all-but-uttered, and yet out of reach.

Whatever god there be, he is, to de la Mare, indwelling. The idea is further enforced when the Traveller, gazing into an "immeasurable well" that is the center of the Eye, seems to see that "a presence there gazed back," which is described as "Rapt, immaterial, remote . . . And yet, in all-embracing consciousness/ Of its own inmost being; elsewise blind." In the midst of this eye, the Traveller sees "a mote scarce visible—Himself." And, although he is "the momentary looking-glass/ Of Nature," from his gaze, "a flame divine burned through" and he has a realization that he is "A son of God—no sport of Time or Fate." But this rapture too is transient, and he dies gasping "Alas!"

"The Traveller," far from being an "affirmation of faith" in a "mysterious, but . . . a pitiful God" affirms an awareness of the transcience of existence which almost approaches despair. A product of his late years, the poem makes it all too apparent that de la Mare had found no happy faith—at least in conventional terms.

An affirmation is expressed in this poem, but it is a relatively bleak
one:

> Ay, what though Man have but one earthly life,
> Cradle to grave, wherein to joy and grieve?
> His grace were yet the agony and strife
> In quest of what no mortal can achieve.

An earlier poem, "The Familiar" (1921) expresses similarly the
idea that the only God there is in man himself; it is an enigmatic
colloquy between the speaker and a Voice that can be taken as
God's. When the speaker asks "Are you far away?" the Voice
answers,

> "Yea, I am far—far;
> Where the green wave shelves to the sand,
> And the rainbows are;
> And an ageless sun beats fierce
> From an empty sky:
> There, O thou Shadow forlorn,
> Is the wraith of thee, I."

However much he might have stated it, life was by no means all
"agony and strife" to de la Mare: beauty and love remain. Perhaps
no other poem captures that belief so well as the magnificent
"Fare Well" (1918) whose last stanza could easily be said to express the faith by which he lived and which is embodied in all of
his poetry:

> Look thy last on all things lovely,
> Every hour. Let no night
> Seal thy sense in deathly slumber
>   Till to delight
> Thou have paid thy utmost blessing;
> Since that all things thou wouldst praise
> Beauty took from those who loved them
>   In other days.[6]

And in 1918 de la Mare wrote in "The Tryst": "Somewhere
there Nothing is; and there lost Man/ Shall win what changeless
vague of peace he can."

III *The Supernatural*

The term "supernatural" is an uneasy one to apply to a great area of Walter de la Mare's interest if it is taken to mean "Of, or proceeding from, an order of existence beyond nature, or the visible and observable universe." For de la Mare, there could have been nothing "beyond nature"; and, as his essays testify, he had on many occasions seen or felt the presence of "ghosts," "shadows," "spectres." The testimony is also in his prose tales and especially in his poetry. He felt that these presences are everywhere, but they are not necessarily departed spirits or malign influences. More often than not, "ghost" in de la Mare's terms is more closely to be identified with the Anglo-Saxon word from which it derives: *gāst,* spirit, soul, breath.

It can be as immaterial as the presence felt when two friends talk; when

> Between the grace-notes of
> The voice of love
> From each to each
> Trembles a rarer speech,
> And with its presence every pause doth fill.
>   ("Silence")

In such poems, the presence bespeaks love; but there are other times when the presence, though equally immaterial, seems foreboding and terrible. Such is the case in "Winter Dusk," a lovely narrative of a mother reading to her two children: "Nor dreamed she, as she read to two,/ 'Twas surely three who heard." Still she seems to know of, to intuit, the presence of the undreamed of, unseen intruder:

> Yet when, the story done, she smiled
> From face to face, serene and clear,
> A love, half dread, sprang up, as she
> Leaned close and drew them near.

Ghosts or spirits are often encountered in sleep and are often more material than mere "felt" presences. When the body, which de la Mare considered as an habitation, is asleep, the spirit goes

forth; or, as he says it in "The Flight," "When the world's clocks
are dumb in sleep/ 'Tis then I seek my kind." Again, his prose as
well as his poetry gives abundant evidence that he believed that
all mankind—all birds and beasts, too, for that matter—have,
asleep, two worlds:

> a globe forgot
> Wheeling from dark to light;
> And all the enchanted realm of dream
> That burgeons out of night.
>
> ("Sleep")

In de la Mare's world, not only is every creature inhabited by a
spirit but every house, every garden, every place where man has
been at one time retains ghosts, presences; and, in his most an-
thologized poem, he calls them "listeners." When one talks of a
house having "personality," one is saying in a rather commonplace
way what de la Mare felt was true in the deepest sense. Surely, we
have all at one time or another visited an ancient structure—Ver-
sailles, the Parthenon, Chartres—and felt the presence of those
who were there long before us. De la Mare shares in this feeling,
but he differs in that he endowed these presences with more reality than most other people are likely to do. "Breathe not—trespass
not" the poet warns in "The Sunken Garden,"

> Of this green and darkling spot, . . .
> Perchance a distant dreamer dreams;
> Perchance upon its darkening air,
> The unseen ghosts of children fare.

In "Vacant Farmhouse" the speaker describes first the house,
then the garden about it whose fruit trees are now "suckered,
rank, unpruned," and finally the abandoned out-buildings. Then
his eye travels back to the house:

> That attic casement. . . . Was there a flaw in the glass? . . .
> I thought, as I glanced up, there had peered a face.
> But no. Still: eyes are strange; for at my steady stare
> Through the cool sunlit evening air,

[58]

> Scared silent sparrows flew up out of the ivy there
> Into an elder tree—for perching-place.

Again, there is the suggestion of a spirit or spectre in the house, but the poem also suggests there may be something spectre-ish about the speaker himself. If this is so, the idea appears many times in de la Mare's work: "The Revenant," for example, claims that "Men all are shades."

Perhaps the most delightful poem of this nature is one of his poems for children, "The Old Stone House." In it he captures the feeling of terror, and curiosity, that all children have when they must pass a house that is haunted:

> Nothing on the grey roof, nothing on the brown,
> Only a little greening where the rain drips down;
> Nobody at the window, nobody at the door,
> Only a little hollow which a foot once wore;
> But still I tread on tiptoe, still tiptoe on I go,
> Past nettles, porch, and weedy well, for oh, I know
> A friendless face is peering, and a clear still eye
> Peeps closely through the casement as my step goes by.

Sometimes presences in de la Mare's poems—"The Revenant," "The Ghost," and "Thus Her Tale," for example—are ghosts in the sense that most children think of them: spirits of the dead returning. De la Mare would have been reluctant, however, to accept the concept of the return of a departed spirit because he would have had difficulty believing that spirits depart. Central to his belief in the possibility of ghosts is the belief in what he might have called "the law of conservation of the spirit"—nothing created, nothing destroyed. As J. B. Priestley observed and as has been pointed out elsewhere, de la Mare's world is the region which lies "between the conscious mind of our time and the great deep of the collective unconscious." [7] In that region the self has continual existence—transmuted, to be sure, but always there. In this sense, then, the self neither comes from anywhere nor goes anywhere. It *is*.

IV *The Impossible She*

Unfortunately, as soon as one makes a dogmatic statement about de la Mare, one is forced to deny its validity. There is a spirit, constantly evoked in his work, who seems to have departed. This spirit de la Mare called, on several occasions, the "Impossible She." She walks abroad in his novels and in his tales; and she is ever present in his poetry. The closest relative of the "Impossible She" as I have pointed out earlier, is Shelley's spirit of Intellectual Beauty. But of course her forebears are of a long and illustrious lineage which can be traced with certainty back at least to Plato. One is aware of her presence in all of de la Mare's work. In *The Return* she is "The mystery that haunts both day and night, past all the changing of the restless hours"; she is "the presence, the grave and lovely overshadowing dream whose surrender made life a torment, and death the near fold of an immortal, starry veil." [8] In *The Three Mulla-Mulgars,* she is so beautiful that "A Mulgar who dreams even of one of her Maidens, and wakes still in the presence of his dream, can no longer be happy in the company of his kind." She is, in *At First Sight,* to Cecil, the "phantom of his dreams."

The "Impossible She" is also the inspiration for a considerable number of de la Mare's poems. Traditionally, she might be considered the muse of poetry; certainly as such she is invoked by countless poets. But in de la Mare's work she is considerably more than a conventional figure: she is, perhaps, the Eve that Adam in "The Exile" yearns to re-welcome; when, he pleads, will he "No more with wordless grief a loved one grieve,/ But to Heaven's nothingness re-welcome Eve?" She is that vision whom de la Mare describes in "Vain Finding" as "A beauty beyond earth's content,/ A hope—half memory." She is elusive: "Thee whom I shall never find"; yet she is immortal and changeless:

> All the world's woods, tree o'er tree
> Come to nought.
> Birds, flowers, beasts, how transient they,
> Angels of a flying day.
> Love is quenched; dreams drown in sleep;
> Ruin nods along the deep:

> Only thou immortally
>   Hauntest on
> This poor earth in Time's flux caught;
> Hauntest on, pursued, unwon,
> Phantom child of memory,
>   Beauteous one!
>   ("The Phantom")

As to the identity of the "Impossible She," de la Mare is incon-
clusive: "A thousand cheating names hath she;/ And none foretokens rest" ("The Decoy"). Perhaps she is the Spirit of Air who
"Floats on a cloud and doth ride/ Clad in the beauties of earth/
Like a bride" ("Spirit of Air"). Perhaps she is "The Shade" who
"darkens against the darkness" to whom the speaker pleads, "O
dream, return once more/ To gloomy Hades and the whispering
shore!" Perhaps, instead, she is "my love,/ Lost in far-wandering
desire" who "Hath in the darkling deep above/ Set stars and kin-
dled fire" ("Invocation"). It is possible, too, that she is that Self
for which all men search:

> Lost in heaven's vague, the stars burn softly through
> The world's dark latticings, we prisoned stray
> Within its lovely labyrinth, and know
>   Mute seraphs guard the way
> Even from silence unto speech, from love
> To that self's self it still is dreaming of.
>   ("Nocturne")

Whatever she is, in whatever shape or disguise she visits, she
haunts the work of Walter de la Mare; because of her, he says, in
"Music Unheard": "all I love/ In beauty cries to me,/ 'We but
vain shadows/ And reflections be.'" He suggests she is indwelling: she is "that inward presence" which "slumbers not," in the
poem "Haunted." She is the "life of life" of whom he asks in "The
Strange Spirit,"

> Whose servant art thou? Who gave thee earth, sky and sea
> For uttermost kingdom and ranging? Who bade thee to be
> Bodiless, lovely; snare, and delight of the soul,
> Fantasy's beacon, of thought the uttermost goal?

And in "The Mirage," she is "Beauty inexorable" that has lured men on, whom the poet in this poem names at last—Despair.

Sometimes the poems are not lyrics or invocations addressed to the "Impossible She"; instead, they are narratives dramatizing her power. Such a poem is "Old Angler" from *The Veil* (1921). This poem, an allegory but undistinguished as poetry, is important because it illustrates one of de la Mare's major preoccupations. The angler, fishing, is described as having "in pensive solitariness . . . fished existence by." Suddenly, he feels a tug on the line: his hook has become entangled in the locks of "a wan-pale, lovely" naiad. She circles the boat, uttering "a grieving, desolate wail." The angler, for whom "Long sterile years had come and gone;/ Youth, like a distant dream, was sped;/ Heart, hope, and eyes had hungered on . . ." in compassion draws his knife and cuts the hook from the naiad's hair. Freed, she swims away laughing "a mocking, icy, inhuman note," while the angler

> —the cheated? Dusk till morn,
> Insensate, even of hope forsook,
> He muttering squats, aloof, forlorn,
> Dangling a baitless hook.

"Old Angler" may be an allegory of the poet's life, or perhaps of the life of all men who are enamored of the "Impossible She." It may also be read in symbolic terms: the angler is the man who "fishes" in the waters of the unconscious, who catches the inexpressibly beautiful prize—a momentary realization, a glimpse of truth—but perforce must release it out of common humanity; and who finally recognizes that he has lost the irretrievable.

As I have pointed out elsewhere in this study, water is often a symbol of the unconscious in de la Mare's work, as well as one of life, of time and flux, or of eternity itself. This use of water is apparent in another narrative poem, "The Visionary" in which a "wanderer" stumbles upon a pool in a forest. "Parched, forlorn," he stoops to refresh himself and sees in the water

> A face like amber, pale and still,
> With eyes of light, unchangeable,
> Whose grave and steadfast scrutiny
> Pierced through all earthly memory.

Then, inevitably, although he drinks the water, he cannot possess the face. He goes back to "life's wild banishment"

> Like one whose every thought doth seem
> The wreckage of a wasting dream;
> All savour gone from life, delight
> Charged with forboding dark as night;
> Love but the memory of what
> Woke once, but reawakens not.

It would be easy to find in these poems about the "Impossible She" justification for biographical interpretation. One can hear a student saying "He must have had a love affair and it didn't turn out right." Since I refuse to be either sophomoric or Freudian, I feel that the "Impossible She" in de la Mare's work is that same spirit which haunts all men of feeling, of passion for the beautiful and the good. She is apparent in one form or another in the works of all great poets. De la Mare was able to express it as well as any other—as in his last stanza about a miracle called "The Snowflake":

> Lo, this entranced thing!—a breath
> Of life that bids Man's heart to crave
> Still for perfection: ere fall death,
> And earth shut in his grave.

The "Impossible She," a ghost, a phantom, a spirit—an hallucination, if you will, or a snowflake—has haunted and will continue to haunt those who in this imperfect world crave "still for perfection."

V *Children*

Among Walter de la Mare's best poems are those he wrote for and about children. Of the one hundred forty-eight first and revised editions of his work catalogued in a checklist compiled by the National Book League in 1956, over thirty-five entries are the names of books of children's poems. His first published collection, *Songs of Childhood* (1902), indicated an interest in children which was to be life-long. In 1919 he was to collaborate with a thirteen-year-old artist, Pamela Bianco, by writing poems to illustrate her drawings. In 1925 Ellen Terry was to make her last appearance in *Crossings: A Fairy Play,* which he had first published in 1921. "A collection of rhymes and poems for the young of all ages" called *Come Hither,* the first of his five creative anthologies, appeared in 1925; and ten years later another such volume, *Early One Morning in the Spring. Chapters on Children and on Childhood as it is revealed in particular in Early Memories and in Early Writings,* was published. These and all the other editions not named here; his novel, *The Three Mulla-Mulgars;* and his countless stories for children—among the most delightful of which are collected in *Broomsticks* (1925)—attest to his abiding interest in the young.

Yet never once to my knowledge does de la Mare patronize or, for that matter, idealize children. They are from his point of view neither miniature, and therefore rather dull, adults—nor sage philosophers and seers blessed. And his interest in childhood was not the result of an escape mechanism; or, if it were, it is not apparent in his work. His poems reflect his fascination and delight in children and, even more apparently, his knowledge of them. He seems to know almost instinctively what appeals to them, as well as what they are really like.

What child is not delighted by rhythmic sound: " 'Grill me some bones,' said the Cobbler"; "Whsst, and away and over the green,/ Scampered a shape that was never seen"; "Old Tillie Turveycombe/ Sat to sew"; "Far away in Nanga-noon/ Lived an old and grey Baboon"; "Slowly, silently, now the moon/ Walks the night in her silver shoon." The sounds enchant. But it is not for the sounds only that de la Mare's rhymes and verses captivate children. They can be as grizzly and terrible as any child could wish; an understated horror, however, enhances their terror. "At the Keyhole," of which " 'Grill me some bones,' said the Cobbler," is the first line, is an outstanding example of this technique. Another even more subtle one is "I Can't Abear":

> I can't abear a Butcher,
>   I can't abide his meat,
> The ugliest shop of all is his,
>   The ugliest in the street;
> Bakers' are warm, cobblers' dark

> Chemists' burn watery lights;
> But oh, the sawdust butcher's shop,
> That ugliest of sights!

In such a poem the speaker does not need to tell what the sights are. Any child hearing or reading "I Can't Abear" can imagine them—that is, any child who has ever seen anything other than pre-packaged, supermarket meat.

But although de la Mare sometimes assumes the point of view of a child, he also comments upon a child's fascination with bloodshed and death. "Dry August Burned" is such a comment. In it a small child has seen a newly-shot hare lying on the kitchen table, and she "wept out her heart to see it there." Soon, the sound of soldiers on their way to maneuvers in a field nearby interrupts her weeping. She runs out-of-doors to watch them pass,

> And then—the wonder and the tumult gone—
> Stood nibbling a green leaf, alone,
> Her dark eyes, dreaming. . . . She turned, and ran,
> Elf-like, into the house again

and into the kitchen where she finds her mother. The devastating conclusion to the poem comes as the child, "her tear-stained cheek now flushed with red," looks for the rabbit and asks her mother, "Please, may I go and see it skinned?"

Of course, "Dry August Burned" is about more than one child, and the situation can be generalized to have far greater significance than that of a child discovering the fascination of death. The initial impact worn off: "Mother, then what happens?" is the child's normal response. The poem also shows that de la Mare's vision of childhood was not by any means sentimentalized or unrealistic: his appraisal was shrewd.

His genius for seeing and for discovering nature as a child does is apparent in so many of his rhymes that it is difficult to select one or two for purposes of illustration. "Before I melt/ Come, look at me!" cries a newly-fallen snowflake who then goes on to boast,

> Of a great forest
> In one night

WALTER DE LA MARE

I make a wilderness
Of white.

The power of the snowflake established, reality reasserts itself as
the snowflake admits, "Breathe, and I vanish/ Instantly." It is just
a short step in the imagination of a child from the fate of the
snowflake to the fate of all things in a child's world—including
himself. Children do not articulate these feelings because they do
not have the words with which to do so. If one asked a child who
has just breathed upon a snowflake what he is thinking, one could
not possibly expect to have him say, "Oh, I am thinking of the
transience of all things lovely, including myself." But one knows
that in some preternatural way that this is the knowledge that the
child has gained from the experience.

"Seeds" again shows de la Mare's ability to see from the child's
point of view:

> The seeds I sowed—
> For weeks unseen—
> Have pushed up pygmy
> Shoots of green;
> So frail you'd think
> The tiniest stone
> Would never let
> A glimpse be shown.
> But no; a pebble
> Near them lies,
> At least a cherry-stone
> In size,
> Which that mere sprout
> Has heaved away,
> To bask in sunshine,
> See the Day.

Even when he writes as an adult for children, his observations
are just as delightful. For example, there is the first lesson in phys-
iology called "Miss T.":

> It's a very odd thing—
> As odd as can be—
> That whatever Miss T. eats

Turns into Miss T.;
Porridge and apples,
  Mince, muffins and mutton,
Jam, junket, jumbles—
  Not a rap, not a button
It matters; the moment
  They're out of her plate,
Though shared by Miss Butcher
  And sour Mr. Bate;
Tiny and cheerful,
  And neat as can be,
Whatever Miss T. eats
  Turns into Miss T.

And then there is the rhyme about Old King Caraway who "supped on cake,/ And a cup of sack" and who would

nibble and sip
While his dreams slipped by;
And when he had finished,
  He'd nod and say,
"Cake and sack
  For King Caraway!"

Occasionally, de la Mare wrote poetic narratives which have the charm of the familiar as well as the magic of something new. Such is the tale, "Sam's Three Wishes." In the first two lines, the fascination begins: "I'm thinking and thinking," said old Sam Shore,/ " 'Twere somebody *knocking* I heard at the door." Of course, it is a good fairy he finds at the door, but not until after an appropriate amount of suspense is engendered. Old Sam Shore is given three wishes: his first is for a goose "to fry in the oven"; his second, for his mother to be back with him for, he tells the fairy, "if there was one thing she couldn't refuse/ 'Twas a sweet thick slice from the breast of a goose." His old mother appears: "Why, Sam," says she, "the bird be turning,/ For my nose tells I that the skin's a-burning!" Sam's third and final wish is that both he and his mother return to their youth—a wish which the fairy grants, and Sam is once again a boy and his mother young. The tale continues and they get older; his mother dies, and Sam is once again Old

Sam. One night as he sits in his lonely cottage "gloomily gooming" at his meager dinner, he hears something at the door:

> soft as a rattle counting her seeds
> In the midst of a tangle of withered-up-weeds—
> Came a faint, faint knocking, a rustle like silk,
> And a breath at the keyhole as soft as milk—
> Still as the flit of a moth. And then . . .
> That infinitesimal knocking again.

It is, one can surmise, the good fairy again, for the poet's *envoi* begins: "But if Sam's story you'd read to the end./ Turn back to page 1, and press onward, dear friend"; and it concludes with an observation de la Mare made many times over in other contexts: "For all sober records of life (come to write 'em)/ Are bound to continue—well—ad infinitum!" Such a conclusion is guaranteed to send any child's mind and many adult's back to "page 1" again and again—ad infinitum.

A child's mind is uncluttered; it is occupied with the elemental things to which it attends with unwavering, though brief, concentration. Truly Blakean, de la Mare knew what it was to "see a world in a grain of sand" and knew that this is the way children see. But, although a child's imagination can see "eternity in an hour," it can also see without comprehension the realities of existence—among which one must include death. In "Peeping Tom" this blindness—a blessing of innocence, perhaps—is illustrated. The speaker is a young child;

> I was there—by the curtains
> When some men brought a box
> And one at the house of
>   Miss Emily knocks.

He reports seeing the strange men go into Miss Emily's house, for what reason he does not surmise and confesses

>   why all her blinds
> Have been hanging so low
> These dumb foggy days
> I don't know.

Only last week, he says, he saw her "potting out for the winter her / Balcony flowers," and just this Sunday

> She mused there a space,
> Gazing into the street, with
>   The vacantest face.
> Then turned her long nose,
> And looked up at the skies—
> One you would not have thought
>   Weather-wise!

The departure of the men from Miss Emily's house returns him to the present. He notices them as they "climbed to their places . . . In their square varnished carriage"; and, after they have gone from sight,

> Then the road became quiet:
> Her house stiff and staid—
> Like a Stage while you wait
>   For the Harlequinade . . .

And again his thoughts return to Miss Emily and what he has just seen transpire. And he wonders:

> But what can Miss Emily
> Want with a box
> So long, narrow, shallow,
>   And without any locks?

Thus a child without the knowledge of what drawn curtains, and "long, narrow, shallow," lockless boxes mean, must be. But the poem, "Peeping Tom" also demonstrates the subtlety of de la Mare's technique. Its title, for example, is not suggestive of innocence. The child is a peeping tom, but ironically not upon a scene that such creatures are likely to look. The child's point of view is retained in the adjective "dumb" which modifies "foggy days," for it is typically a favorite epithet in a child's vocabulary. Yet here again there is another meaning of which the child is not aware: stillness, death. Then as the child remembers her only last week "potting . . . her balcony flowers" for the winter, irony again subtly tells the truth; a truth which is enforced in the following stanza when she is seen musing, "with the vacantest face." And the fact that she is musing on a Sunday is suggestive of the vanity of the Christian myth. Notice the difference it would have made had the poet chosen Monday or Tuesday as the day on which the child caught her musing.

What she is musing about might be suggested in the next stanza when the child, observing her looking up at the sky, says she is not "one you would . . . have thought/ Weather-wise!" Perhaps, the reader thinks, Miss Emily was weather-wise, and the portents that she saw and about which she was musing were prognostications of her own death. In the next to the last stanza, when the men have left and the road is quiet, the child sees her house as "stiff and staid"—certainly as Miss Emily was while alive—and then when it is compared to a "Stage while you wait/ For the Harle-quinade" the child almost seems to be as a god looking upon the stage of the world, waiting for the show to begin again. But the suggestion is dismissed, and the reader returns to the child's mind, which wonders, bemused, "But what can Miss Emily/ Want with a box . . . ?"

"Peeping Tom" is by no means an unusual poem in the de la Mare canon. Many of them are deceptively simple, especially when they are for children or are written from a child's point of view. But, more than likely, they record the deepest mysteries of life and death.

De la Mare also sees children from an adult point of view and especially later in life the tone of his poetry is tinged with nostal-gia, as is obvious in his brief portrait of "A Child Asleep":

> Angel of Words, in vain I have striven with thee,
> Nor plead a lifetime's love and loyalty;
> Only, with envy, bid thee watch this face,
>   That says so much, so flawlessly,
>   And in how small a space!

Also about a little girl, the poem, "Pollie," shows the speaker giving her lessons. He is certain that "Pollie is a simpleton," for "Every lesson I allot,/ As soon as learned is clean forgot." She can not even learn to spell "love." The last stanza, however, moves away from amused and affectionate exasperation:

> It seems in her round head you come
> As if to a secret vacuum;
> Whence then the wonder, love and grace
> Shining in that small face?

In another poem, "Brother and Sister," from the same collection, *Memory* (1938), the speaker muses upon the fact that both he and his beloved sister have grown old. His love for her makes him see her as still beautiful, with a beauty enhanced by the wisdom she has acquired. Yet, the speaker concludes: "had I Prospero's wizardry/ She should at once have back her youth,/ Whatever chanced to me." Occasionally, then, the poet seems to regret the loss of childhood. In "In A Library," for example, the speaker longs for a book "To teach an old man/ To teach himself." Were he to find such a book, he would be "Even with self reconciled"; for, reading it, he would be "Retrieving the wisdom" he lost "when a child." Relatively few, however, are the poems which look somewhat wistfully and longingly at that lost paradise, that "pre-Edenic" peace that childhood was, or that an aging adult might think it was. To emphasize them would be a disservice to the great bulk of his rhymes and verses for children, many of which have already become classics:

> Ann, Ann!
> Come! quick as you can!
> There's a fish that *talks*
> In the frying-pan.

This one poem is enough to endear de la Mare to all children.

VI *Nature*

Perhaps de la Mare's "curious bias towards the miniature," as Lord David Cecil calls it,[9] was responsible in part for his interest in children and in other small creatures. Certainly, one must agree with E. V. Knox that de la Mare was never "greatly interested in elephants," [10] for a survey of his poetry which is primarily concerned with nature will reveal not one elephant but countless wrens, titmice, violets, bluebells, snails, and flies. Mr. Knox was being amusing in making this remark, I am sure; but I am also sure that, if elephants roamed England and were part of an ordinary Englishman's experience, de la Mare would have written many poems about them. For above all, his landscape is as English as the creatures who inhabit it are. And, if nothing else, de la Mare's nature poetry is a monumental testimony to his powers of observation—to his ability to attend to the ordinary with extraordinary perception. Here, for example, is "Jenny Wren,"

> Never was sweeter seraph hid
> Within so small a house—
> A tiny, inch-long, eager, ardent
> Feathered mouse.

And here is "The Snail":

> All day shut fast in whorled retreat
> You slumber where—no wild bird knows;
> While on your rounded roof-tree beat
> The petals of a rose.

These are England's creatures to whom de la Mare has attended. But surely everywhere the wren is a "tiny inch-long eager, ardent/ Feathered mouse," and the snail's house has a "rounded roof-tree"; just as "Old ashen rooks, on ragged wing" have "heads with sidling eye." Such felicity for finding the perfect word to describe is not rare in de la Mare.

But, however acute his powers of observation and attention, de la Mare seldom rested in mere description of nature. He was rarely a mere observer because he felt so deeply that all living things share the common mystery. Furthermore, he was convinced that this involvement was shared not only by all living creatures but by all of nature. "The Snowdrop" suggests the primary motive for his focusing of attention on all natural things:

> Now—now, as low I stooped, thought I
> I will see what this snowdrop *is;*

> So shall I put much argument by,
>   And solve a lifetime's mysteries.

His first quest, here as in other situations, is to find some solution to "a lifetime's mysteries." He goes on in this poem to show what he discovered in this particular instance:

> Mind fixed, but else made vacant, I,
> Lost to my body, called my soul
> To don that frail solemnity
>   Its inmost self my goal.
> And though in vain—no mortal mind
> Across that threshold yet hath fared!—
> In this collusion I divined
>   Some consciousness we shared.

To de la Mare, all of earth's inhabitants, animate or inanimate, share "some consciousness"; for they all have, at least, the same fate—as in the "Titmouse" at a feeding station:

> This tiny son of life; this spright; . . .
> Plume will his wing in the dappling light,
> Clash timbrel shrill and gay—
> And into Time's enormous Nought,
>   Sweet-fed will flit away.

Not just snowdrops and birds, however, share with man the inevitability of the journey into "Time's enormous Nought." Here in the same vein is the last stanza of "A Rose in Candlelight":

> Lo, now, the light that bathes this rose,
> That wondrous red its cheek to give!
> It breathes, "We, too, a secret share;
> Fleeting we are, however fair;
> And only representative."

Of what the light and the rose are representatives, de la Mare does not suggest in this or in any other poem. Instead, he characteristically questions, in "The Miracle,"—"Who beckons the green ivy up/ Its solitary tower of stone?"—and gives no answer. For the universe is to him indifferent; and all its creatures share the common fate. Even flowers, for example:

> Flowers in silent desire
>   Their life-breath exhale—
> Self-heal, hellebore, aconite,
>   Chamomile, dwale:
> Sharing the same gentle heavens,
>   The sun's heat and light,
> And, in the dust at their roots
>   The same shallow night.
>
>   ("The Bottle")

And man fares no better: "Prove thou thy lordship who hadst dust for nurse/ And for thy swaddling the primal mire," he mocks in "Humanity."

The poem that states most clearly the involvement of all nature in what is, ultimately, an indifferent universe, is "Immanent" from the 1953 volume, *O Lovely England:*

> The drone of war-plane neared, and dimmed away;
> The child, above high-tide mark, still toiled on.
> Salt water welled the trench that in his play
> He'd dug as moat for fort and garrison.
>
> Lovely as Eros, and half-naked too,
> He heaped dried beach-drift, kindled it, and lo!
> A furious furnace roared, the sea winds blew . . .
> Vengeance divine! And death to every foe!
>
> Young god!—and not ev'n Nature eyed askance
> The fire-doomed Empire of a myriad Ants.

As this poem so ironically underlines, the microcosm to de la Mare is a reflection of the macrocosm: the indifference of the child, reflected in the indifference of mankind to life, is in itself merely a reflection of the supreme indifference of Nature.

However impersonal and unconcerned the universe, man himself need not be. This de la Mare most emphatically believed, and he was vehement in his denunciation of man's cruelty to his fellow creatures. "Considering how man has treated the animals, isn't it surprising that any animal should trust him?" he once remarked in conversation;[11] and this observation is a preoccupation in many of his poems. In "Hi!" for example, his tone is savagely denunciatory:

> Hi! handsome hunting man
> Fire your little gun.
> Bang! Now the animal
> Is dead and dumb and done.
> Never more to peep again, creep again, leap again,
> Eat or sleep or drink again. Oh, what fun!

A similar observation and tone are to be found in "Tit for Tat" in which he envisions the huntsman and his quarry as having reversed roles. Ostensibly for children, this poem should give the most callous adult pause. Addressing himself to Tom Noddy, the speaker asks how the hunting is:

> Have you trod like a murderer through the green woods . . .
> While every small creature screamed shrill to Dame Nature,
> "He comes—and he comes!"

The speaker then suggests to Tom that perhaps one day, while he is hunting, "An Ogre from space will stoop a lean face/ And lug you home." The speaker then imagines what will happen to Tom. The Ogre will

> Lug you home over his fence, Tom Noddy,
>   Of thorn-sticks nine yards high,
> With your bent knees strung round his old iron gun
>   And your head dan-dangling by:
>
> And hang you up stiff on a hook, Tom Noddy,
>   From a stone-cold pantry shelf,
> Whence your eyes will glare in an empty stare,
>   Till you are cooked yourself!

Savage though he can be concerning man's indifference to his fellow creatures, de la Mare often looks with humor and with a wry good will at the kinship with them which underlies man's brief sojourn on earth. Such, for example, is the poem "Comfort" in which a man and his cat, seated before the fire, share the warm solitude. The cat speaks,

> "Dear God, what security,
>   Comfort and bliss!
> And to think, too, what ages,
>   Have brought us to this!"

What the cat means by "this" is revealed in the next stanza:

> "You in your sheep's-wool coat,
>   Buttons of bone,
> And me in my fur-about
>   On the warm hearthstone."

Here, as he often does, de la Mare laughs at the pretentions of man who has come, how many countless ages, to this comfort, this security, this bliss—"a sheep's-wool coat" with "buttons of bone" —while the cat has always had its "fur-about." The underlying irony in the situation is, of course, that the "comfort and bliss" of both man and beast are so ephemeral.

More often than not de la Mare's nature poetry confirms what he wrote in "Nobody Knows": "And so we live under deep water/ All of us, beasts and men." But this is no answer to the mystery, nor did he mean it to be. Simply stated, the reason that it is not the answer is found in "Mrs. Earth":

> Mrs. Earth makes silver black,
>   Mrs. Earth makes iron red,
> But Mrs. Earth cannot stain gold
>   Nor ruby red.
> Mrs. Earth the slenderest bone,
>   Whitens in her bosom cold,
> But Mrs. Earth can change my dreams
>   No more than ruby or gold.
> Mrs. Earth and Mr. Sun
>   Can tan my skin, and tire my toes,
> But all that I'm thinking of, ever shall think,
>   Why, neither knows.

Involved as we all are in time, and ruthless though it may be, de la Mare looks upon it in "The Moment" with some compassion:

> O Time—the heedless child you are!
> A daisy, the most distant star
> Fall to your toying scimitar.
>
> And I. And this loved face? We too
> Are things but of a moment. True:
> But then, poor youngling, so are you!
>
> Dream on! In your small company
> We are contented merely to be—
> Yes, even to Eternity.

Thus, along with Mrs. Earth and Mr. Sun, even time itself shares in the eternal mystery; and the solution to it—time, man, nature will never know.

CHAPTER 5

The Novels:
The Pilgrimage of the Imagination

BECAUSE the period in which the novels of Walter de la Mare were published began in 1904 and ended in 1928, he can be considered as a latter-day Victorian or as a Georgian. He claimed an affinity with Hardy insofar as his concept of God is concerned;[1] and his prose style and the themes of some of his short stories reveal the influence of Henry James, particularly of "The Turn of the Screw," and "The Sacred Fount."[2] Also Joseph Conrad's probings of the nature of good and evil, and W. H. Hudson's observations of nature can be said to have exerted an influence on de la Mare's imagination.[3]

But, as I have pointed out elsewhere, the real seeds of his art were planted long before any of these writers existed—in Plato's Theory of Ideas. This is not to say that the influence of Plato on de la Mare was direct, for it is a truism to state that any person who believes that the phenomenal world is not the true reality, that neither sensations nor words can furnish a knowledge of this reality, and that what is real can be apprehended only by the imagination—"reason," to use Plato's term—is a follower of the Greek philosopher.

Another compelling influence upon de la Mare is what can be termed the delight of the English temperament in fantasy, faerie, and the supernatural. Whether this proclivity can be attributed to the Celtic strain in the British, as Matthew Arnold avers in his lecture "On the Study of Celtic Literature," is not necessary to determine; for it can be discerned in every epoch throughout the history of British literature. Many of de la Mare's contemporaries were mining this rich vein: H. G. Wells's fantasies appeared in quick succession during the period 1895-1908; and at approximately the same time E. M. Forster's "Celestial Omnibus" and some of the tales which were to be collected in The Eternal Mo-

ment and Other Stories were appearing. The decade of the 1920's saw the publication of fantasies such as T. F. Powys' *Mr. Weston's Good Wine*, Ronald Fraser's *The Flying Draper*, David Garnett's *Lady into Fox* and *A Man in the Zoo*, and many others by less well-known writers.

Sometimes the element of fantasy is grounded in reality and used for satiric purposes as in Swift's *Gulliver's Travels*, Butler's *Erewhon*, Forster's "The Machine Stops," or Huxley's *Brave New World*. At other times fantasies like George Abbott's *Flatland* translate the phenomenal world into one that would be the delight of any Pythagorean; or, as in the case of Lewis Carroll's adventures of Alice, into a world completely the reverse of the one of ordinary perception. And, finally, fantasies sometimes appear which suggest that the world of sensation scarcely exists at all, as in the novels of George MacDonald (1824-1905) and Charles Williams (1886-1945). This genre can be called the literature of dream, and it is in this category of fantasy that the bulk of the prose fiction of de la Mare falls.

Of course, correspondences can be found in de la Mare's novels with novels in the first two categories: Carroll's understanding and love of children and delight in nonsense; and Swift's ease in assuming unusual points of view, for instance. And—although traces of Bunyan, Defoe, Blake, the Brontës, and many others can be found in de la Mare—it is to the novels of George MacDonald that one must look for the closest parallel to his themes and methods.

In fact, there can be no doubt that MacDonald's novels exercised a profound influence upon Walter de la Mare, as they did upon Charles Williams, whose first novel, *War in Heaven*, appeared two years after de la Mare had ceased to write long prose fiction. The difference between the two writers lies in the fact that Williams caught the religious impulse fundamental to MacDonald, whereas de la Mare did not. Writing as a critic of de la Mare's poetry, Williams pointed to the paradox that, although it is possible to term de la Mare a religious poet, he seldom invokes God or utilizes the symbols or ideas of any recognizable religion. Williams also notes that de la Mare does not give a philosophy in his poetry. It is fair to assume that Williams would have agreed that de la Mare did neither in his prose fiction. De la Mare differs from

MacDonald and Williams, then, in that he is neither a religious nor a philosophical novelist.

Another obvious dissimilarity between MacDonald's novels and those of de la Mare is that most of MacDonald's lose all touch with the world of sense perception, as in *Phantastes* and *Lilith,* but most of de la Mare's short stories and at least three of his five novels are securely anchored in reality. The two exceptions among the novels are *Henry Brocken* (1904) and *The Three Mulla-Mulgars* (1910). In both of these fantasies, one can discern the influence of MacDonald's *Phantastes;* for in both the central characters embark upon a pilgrimage, as does the hero of *Phantastes;* and in *Henry Brocken* de la Mare follows MacDonald's lead in the use of pertinent epigraphs to head each chapter. The fundamental difference, however, is that *Phantastes* purports to tell of a spiritual pilgrimage into the "fairy Kingdom of Heaven" [4] but that Henry Brocken's travels are to no such goal. Although it has been said that the journey to heaven is the theme of de la Mare's *The Three Mulla-Mulgars,*[5] I feel certain that, although de la Mare was presenting a story of a spiritual pilgrimage, its goal was not the kingdom of Heaven but the realm of imagination. In a word, where MacDonald is religious, perhaps Neo-Platonic, de la Mare is Platonic.

The three de la Mare novels which most nearly approach dream literature, and yet depart from MacDonald's insofar as they are more firmly anchored in what is commonly called reality, are *The Return* (1910), *Memoirs of a Midget* (1921), and *At First Sight* (1928). In each of these novels, the characters are recognizably real people; even the Midget and her hunchback lover, Mr. Anon, are credible in terms of actual experience. Also, in these novels, the settings are suggestive of late Victorian England. MacDonald's settings, on the other hand, are fairy-land, as in *Phantastes* and *A Double Story,* or the House of Death, as in *Lilith.* His characters, too, are almost completely dream symbols: the Wise Woman, in *A Double Story;* or Mara and Lona, in *Lilith,* for example. When MacDonald does shift into the world of actuality, his transitions from one world to another are too obvious to sustain a sense of wonder and mystery, and his religious convictions lead him to moralize. Neither of these shortcomings does de la Mare exhibit. For these reasons, one could with more felicity apply Grenville MacDonald's epithet of "bi-local existence" to de la Mare than, as he does, to his father, George MacDonald.[6] The phenomenal world and one of the imagination are inseparable to de la Mare; he slips easily and secretly through the gates of one into the other and back again; and he takes his readers just as effortlessly with him.

Besides the strains of Platonic thought and of fantasy in his novels, de la Mare shows profound interest in and understanding of children—a characteristic more apparent, it is true, in his poems and short stories. But this awareness of children is also found in the novels, especially in the two early fantasies and to a certain extent in the *Memoirs*. His interest in children is suggestive of Blake and Lewis Carroll, as well as of Christina Rossetti and Charles Kingsley.[7] Many of de la Mare's finest lyrics owe their debt to Blake and Christina Rossetti. And, as in the case of Lewis Carroll and Charles Kingsley, at least one of his novels was written expressly for children.

These writers, in one form or another, recaptured a vision of the world they knew when they were young, and some of them can be said never to have lost the vision throughout their lives: certainly this can be said of Blake and of de la Mare. But it is as much of a mistake to say that de la Mare is primarily the poet or prophet of childhood as it is to say that Blake is, for childhood is just one of the worlds in which they were at ease. Neither Blake, whose point of view was profoundly to influence de la Mare, nor de la Mare was circumscribed by it; for both knew that the only reality was in the mind—in the world of the imagination. The rational world of science had little to offer them, or they to it. Paradoxically, de la Mare's restless and inquiring mind might have contributed much to science, had it also been able to accept the necessary discipline. Perhaps the sense of mystery all children have about the world is lost to them when they grow to know the names of everything, as one recent philosopher has suggested.[8] If this be so, still it cannot be inferred that de la Mare lacked extensive knowledge of the names of things. But, because he believed in the reality of the imagination, he used words, not as the scientist does "to vivisect experience, killing it for the sake of generalized knowledge," but "to capture experience alive." [9]

These, then, are the three main streams of thought to be found in the novels of Walter de la Mare. Idealism and a belief in the supremacy of the imagination is the major theme. Complementing this concept is the willingness to employ fantasy and its adjuncts, occult and supernatural lore, and an awareness of the visionary world of childhood and of dreams. As will be seen, none of these is mutually exclusive; in the novels one or another may predominate but all contribute to de la Mare's search for reality which is, he thought, the imagination.

It is possible that Walter de la Mare's reputation as a poet, a short story writer, and an anthologist has obscured the worth of his novels. But it is also possible that his novels do not appeal to scholars because to apply any intellectually oriented standard of criticism to them is virtually impossible. They are, in great part at least, puzzling because they must be read and understood intuitively; and, although I make no claim to an intuition keener than that possessed by many careful readers, I am convinced that the few commentators who have discussed one or the other of the novels are either misguided in their findings or have ignored or twisted the evidence given in them to arrive at their conclusions. For just as surely as the *Memoirs of a Midget* is not an ingenious commentary upon the plight of the individual versus society, so *The Return* is not merely an exercise upon the Dr. Jekyll-Mr. Hyde theme. I believe also that *Henry Brocken* is more than a fantasy about a bookish child given to dreaming; that *The Three Mulla-Mulgars* does not merely concern itself with the adventures of three monkeys; and that de la Mare's last novel, *At First Sight*, should not be read merely as a boy-meets-girl, boy-loses-girl romantic tragedy.

I will attempt to explore the meaning of the five novels of Walter de la Mare in the belief that each of them presents a particular aspect of his search for the ultimate reality. Starting with the premise that truth is least dependent upon matters of fact or physical circumstance, his was a spiritual or mental quest. The first cause, the unmoved mover, was to him the imagination. Thus the territory he explored is the "little nowhere of the mind" where the imagination exists and the spirit has its being.

The first romance, *Henry Brocken* (1904), examines the creative imagination, while *The Three Mulla-Mulgars* (1910) is a parable of the experience of life and presents the quest for the inexpressible in which the imagination is everlastingly engaged. With *The Return* (1910) the supremacy of the imagination is established and a new and more personal note is sounded, for here love becomes part of the theme. In this novel love is found to be an aspect of the imagination for through its power reality is found, however briefly. The last two novels are informed by this belief. The central character of *Memoirs of a Midget* (1921) achieves knowledge of the ultimate reality with indifferent success because she fails to find the key to the final door. It is not that she lacks the capacity to love; her failure is in her inability to recognize that the ultimate Self is to be found in the imaginative union of two selves. The final novel, *At First Sight* (1928), overcomes this deficiency. Here love is the ultimate imaginative experience because it is shared. But for de la Mare the tragedy of life lies in the fact that, like the mystical experience, the union of two imaginations is momentary. Nevertheless, for a little while the lovers know reality as it truly is. And that is all that, perhaps, anyone can know.

Thus, Walter de la Mare came full circle to his original premise. Reality is the imagination, but in life reality can be only briefly known. Perhaps this is one of the reasons he abandoned the novel form: it may have been an uncongenial tool with which to recreate his vision because of demands of length. Another reason may have been his realization of the limitations of language, for: "Life, in its essence, . . . is as far beyond the reach of words as death is. . . ." [10]

CHAPTER 6

Henry Brocken:
The Journey Begins

W HILE still a clerk in the London offices of the Anglo-American Oil Company, Walter de la Mare completed his first novel—written, incidentally, on the note paper of his employers.[1] In *Henry Brocken*,[2] de la Mare did two things: he explored reality as it is projected by the creative imagination; and he traced the development of the imagination in a child.

The central character, a young child whose name gives the novel its title, mounts a horse early one morning and travels to the lands peopled by characters from his favorite reading. He meets among others, Lucy Gray, Jane Eyre, Sleep and Death, and Criseyde. Not one of the people he encounters is an original creation of de la Mare's—even Henry's horse is borrowed, for its name is Rosinante. On such a journey as this one, however, the name is appropriate for it connotes romance. But Rosinante can also be a symbol of the imagination, as old as Pegasus. The hero of George MacDonald's *Phantastes* might have suggested something to de la Mare, for he also rides a steed in his journey to Fairy-land.[3]

The temptation to suggest that in *Henry Brocken* de la Mare was pouring new wine into old bottles is difficult to resist but for the fact that the usual connotations of that saying concerning the quality of the result are not true in this case. It could not have been de la Mare's intention merely to reanimate the characters of other authors or to reshape them in the same mold in which they were originally cast. It would have been impossible to do. Furthermore, had it been possible, what would have been his reason for doing so? It is more likely that de la Mare felt that these characters were living beings in their own right, endowed with as much if not more reality than ordinary people; for they were, after all, creations of the imagination.

E. M. Forster's remarks on Lowes Dickinson's *The Magic Flute* and James Joyce's *Ulysses* are in a sense applicable to *Henry Brocken:* "Parody or adaptation have enormous advantages to certain novelists, particularly to those who may have a great deal to say and plenty of literary genius, but who do not see the world in terms of individual men and women—who do not, in other words, take easily to creating characters. How are such men to start writing? An already existing book or literary tradition may inspire them—they may find high up in its cornices a pattern that will serve as a beginning, they may swing about on its rafters and gain strength." [4] It was not one but many sources that de la Mare adopted in this first novel. They served him as a kind of beginning. The characters were already alive; but, because his imagination transmuted its raw materials, the characters are recreated.

What de la Mare does is to meet the characters on their own terms—in their own realities, as it were. Sometimes what he sees is very similar to the original, as in the *Pilgrim's Progress* episode. In other cases, they are extensions of the originals, as in the Jane Eyre episode where Brocken encounters Jane and Rochester living years and years after Charlotte Brontë left them to make their own way. Again, as in the meeting with Night and her twin sons, Sleep and Death, de la Mare takes the merest hint from Shelley and then creates what amount to completely original characters. And finally, in still other encounters, notably the Gulliver episode and the meeting with Criseyde, de la Mare departs from the originals and either endows them with the personality that is hinted at in the originals or makes them over into something completely different. Thus, for instance, Gulliver is the irredeemable misanthrope that Swift implies he becomes in the voyage to Houyhnhnmland while, conversely, Yahoos become creatures more to pity than to loathe. By the same alchemy, Criseyde is not the thoroughly anti-romantic realist that Chaucer made her to be. To de la Mare, this type of person could not live at all since such people have no imagination. She has learned, de la Mare implies, that without dreams life is a dreary business. She has learned to long for the inexpressible, perhaps for a hero who will be hers forever. And she even briefly imagines that Henry Brocken may be he.

Henry himself is the only character the author has invented. And critics, from the time of the book's publication, have drawn attention to the fact that Henry is not a convincingly drawn child.

R. L. Megroz noted that Brocken is "an all-seeing ghost." [5] Five years later, Forrest Reid concluded that he "remains a phantom . . . we do not even know whether he is man or boy." [6] And, more recently, Edward Wagenknecht wrote that Henry "seems already a man" by the time he starts on his journey. [7]

But as early as 1904 Francis Thompson, in reviewing *Henry Brocken* had suggested as much. "The idea of childhood is not kept for a single page; he talks and acts as a man in his first encounter." [8] Paradoxically, however, Thompson also stated that Brocken "grows to manhood in his journey." It is unfortunate that Thompson did not develop the latter idea and that other critics failed to recognize its import—or to perceive the fact from a reading of the book itself. Nevertheless, grow is exactly what Henry does; not at all in the physical sense, because he is never described nor is his age disclosed. The growth of Henry's imagination is what is traced.

Years after he had written *Henry Brocken*, de la Mare crystallized his thoughts concerning the development of the imagination in a lecture published in 1919 as *Rupert Brooke and the Intellectual Imagination*. [9] As I have examined this lecture in my chapter on the imagination, I shall only briefly summarize its contents here. The lecture develops the idea that all children are imaginative: when they are very young, their imagination is intuitive, inductive. Children are, in a real sense, visionaries. In growing older, however, the child becomes "transmogrified," and the imagination becomes primarily logical, deductive, and literal. This stage of the imagination, which belongs to boyhood and is called the "intellectual," may completely suppress the visionary imagination of childhood. If it does, the resultant adult has an intellectual imagination; but, if it does not, the child grows into adulthood retaining the attributes of a visionary imagination. A fortunate few possess both types in a heightened degree; and these are the rarest people, of whom, according to de la Mare, Shakespeare was one.

Taking Francis Thompson's statement noted above as a clue, and agreeing that Henry is not a very convincing child, one can read the story and its exploration of reality as an allegory of the development of the mind. If this be so, Henry, throughout the course of his adventures until the last one, is a child in de la

Mare's sense of the word because, regardless of how he speaks, he has the imagination of a child. No one possessing boyhood's logical, intellectual imagination would contemplate such adventures, at least not in the matter-of-course way in which Henry embarks on his; and, to the unimaginative, even recognition that such adventures were possible would be out of the question. There is no suggestion that Henry Brocken or his creator is playing "let's pretend"; and that Henry Brocken remains a child until his last adventure is evident. He is like all children in that he takes entirely for granted not only the situations in which he finds himself but also the people he meets. He goes instantly to the heart of any matter as a child does who, disconcerting though he may be to adults, has not yet learned the rules of "polite" or evasive conversation. In his meeting with Jane Eyre, for instance, this unsophisticated honesty is evident. While Jane plays softly at the piano she asks him almost coquettishly:

"But then, was I not detestable too? so stubborn, so wilful, so demented, so—vain?"

"You were vain," I answered, "because—"

"Well?" she said, and the melody died out, and the lower voices of her music complained softly on.[10]

Henry is a child, too, in his acceptance of the adoration of a Yahoo who dies to save him from the Houyhnhnms, an episode which some may find a rather puzzling reversal of Swift's values. If we agree, however, that children who read *Gulliver's Travels* are not a little shocked by Swift's treatment of creatures in whom they see something of themselves, we can readily understand how Henry might have been repelled by the Yahoos while, at the same time, have been drawn by sympathy to one of the miserable number. So too a child, though overwhelmed by the beauty of the Houyhnhnms, by the "superb freedom of their unbridled heads, the sun-nurtured arrogance of their eyes, the tumultuous, sea-like tossing of crest and tail," could also feel fury at the sight of them: "I lusted to go down and face the mutiny of the brutes; bit, and saddle, and scourge into obedience man's serf of the centuries."[11]

This desire is the first inkling that the child's inheritance as a man is becoming apparent, for as de la Mare has written else-

where: "Man, none too happy even among his own kind, has es-
tranged himself from the inhabitants and habitations of life, its
fauna and flora whose only language is silence, colour, grace,
sweet or raucous noise, the symbols of power, freedom, strangeness and beauty. He is flattered rather than shocked by a tame-
ness in the creatures he has 'domesticated,' which is, after all,
unpleasantly like servility. He enters a wood, and instantly a hos-
tile and vigilant hush intensifies its stillness, such as would fall on
a city at the first windings of the Last Trump." [12]

The episode at World's End, the tavern presided over by Mrs.
Nature and patronized by Mr. Malice, Mr. Liar, and Mr. Pliable
and others of Bunyan's creation, reveals Brocken again as a child
—straightforward, intuitive. Another illustration of his childlike
imagination comes when Henry meets Night and her two sons,
Sleep and Death. Henry is completely unafraid of Death. No one
but a visionary would find Death dark, mysterious, and beautiful:
"no older than the sea, no stranger than the mountains, pure and
cold as the water-springs." Nor would the intellectual imagination
succumb to the invitation of Sleep, while Death looks on envious
of his brother's conquest.

In the final episode, however, Henry undergoes an obvious
change, when despite all counsel to the contrary, he embarks for
the land of Tragedy and there meets Criseyde. "Have you journeyed far?" she asks. "From childhood this side regret," is his answer. "But . . . ," she responds, "you may return, and life heals
every, every wound"; she must remain and make amends. "Tis this
same making amends men now call 'Purgatory,' they tell me." [13]

That Henry is still a child, though "just this side regret," is revealed in his retort: "Amends . . . to whom? For what?" Henry
has begun to question, and soon he will question the sincerity of
Criseyde, who seeks timidly, almost wistfully, to communicate
with him. Chaucer's realist has come to feel loneliness, and she is
beginning to long for something inexpressible. She as much as
warns Henry not to lose the green world of childhood because it is
spiritual death to do so. Henry does not heed her warning. He is,
instead, captivated by the wisdom of a kind other than childhood's, while Criseyde, in turn, seems to have become affected by
his naïveté. She decides "'tis but a little way to being happy—a
touch of the hand, a lifting of the brows, a shuddering silence";

and she impulsively suggests that Henry rescue her: "you shall show me—did one have the wit to learn, and the courage to remember—you shall show me how sails your wonderful little ship," [14]—the little ship of the child's imagination.

Surely this is the plea of the intellectual to the visionary, or of the non-imaginative, perhaps, to the imaginative. But Henry is not equal to the challenge; his newly sprung calculating intellect interferes: "Whom would you seek, did a traveller direct you, and a boat were at your need?" he asks.

> She lowered her lids. "It must be Diomed," she said with the least sigh.
> "It must be," I said.
> "Nay, then, Antenor, or truly Thersites," she said happily, "the silver-tongued!"
> "Good-by, then," I said.
> "Good-by," she replied very gently. [15]

Criseyde becomes a symbol of life itself, and it is Henry's tragedy that he questions and demands that which life cannot give—certainty. The imagination of childhood does not desire maps and charts, nor need affirmation from anything other than itself. Nevertheless, though Henry is undergoing a change, he has not yet become a complete skeptic. Like an "angry child" (the epithet recalls Criseyde's remark that men are "angry boys with beards"), he prepares the boat for her. He fills "the water-keg with fresh water, put fruit and honeycomb and a pillow of leaves into the boat," and leads the lovely woman to it. Henry has one last chance to redeem himself as:

> Criseyde turned from the dark green waves. "Truly, it is a solitary country; pathless," she said, "to one unpiloted;" and stood listening to the hollow voices of the water. And suddenly, as if at the consummation of her thoughts, she lifted her eyes on me, darkly, with unimaginable entreaty.
> "What do you seek else?" I cried in a voice I scarcely recognized.
> "Oh, you speak in riddles!" [16]

The seas of the imagination are pathless. Criseyde needs someone to pilot her, but Brocken will not be he. Henry does not heed

Criseyde's entreaty. He wants to understand her mystery instead of accepting it for what it is. He springs into the boat alone and sails away. But his impatience for answers and his failure to respond to her "unimaginable entreaty" cost him dearly. He leaves the shores he so willingly sought; and, although his boat is buoyant, "how light her cargo!—an oozing honeycomb, ashy fruits, a few branches of drooping leaves, closing flowers; and solitary on the thwart the wraith of life's unquiet dream." [17]

Thus is the voyage of the visionary imagination terminated. The child has journeyed far to experience the tragedy of growing into a manhood whose legacy is "an oozing honeycomb, ashy fruits, a few branches of leaves, closing flowers." It is apparent that what de la Mare was writing in another context can be applied to what Brocken has experienced: ". . . when romance flies out of the window—romance that is as essential to love as expression is to a beautiful face, as music is to a poem—what is called realism comes in at the door." [18] Henry is now an "angry boy with a beard" who will forever make amends for not responding to Criseyde's brief but impassioned entreaty. And life will henceforth be to him, as Death is to Criseyde, an "unquiet dream." [19] Almost as though he had been composing an epitaph for the child, Henry Brocken, de la Mare observed elsewhere: "As we grow older we cannot be content with the certainties of the imagination; we strive intellectually to make assurance doubly sure." [20]

According to his friend Russell Brain, de la Mare was, up to the time of his death, interested in the change that children suffer as they grow. A conversation with de la Mare shows this interest: "He asked whether children did not possess intuition, which they subsequently lost, and, if so, why should they lose it. . . . He thought that children have a perfection of pose and beauty, and natural grace of movement, which they subsequently lose." [21]

Brain also reported that de la Mare's favorite thesis concerning children was that they came into the world fully equipped with a kind of intelligence far superior to any bestowed by experience. [22] And in distinguishing between these two types of intelligence, de la Mare advanced this belief: "There is apprehension . . . and there is comprehension. You have to learn comprehension, but a child often has a very vivid apprehension. Could you tell a man's age from his conversation? And when you say age, which age do

[90]

you mean? Temporal age doesn't count, and perhaps any other kind of age is unreal, if the personality remains the same—if apprehension persists!" [23] This distinction, made late in de la Mare's life, is remarkably consistent to the distinction he made in 1919 between the visionary and the intellectual imagination.

It is evident that Henry Brocken has, in the course of his travels, grown to what will be manhood for him; he has left childhood and arrived at boyhood; his is no longer the visionary's imagination, it is the intellectual's. He has, however, at the outer margin of his imagination met in dream the mysterious "she," who will figure prominently in the later novels, *The Return* and *At First Sight;* and he demands the reassurance she cannot give. She asks: " 'Why, how could there be a vow between us? I go and return. You await me—me, Criseyde, Traveller, the lonely-hearted. That is the little all, O much-surrendering Stranger.' " [24]

Brocken has surrendered much—his powers of apprehension have been submerged by the attempt to comprehend. The child has grown into boyhood, and in his dreams will return, occasionally, Criseyde, who is the mystery: ". . . *l'inconnu,* which Man in his devotion seeks in vain to fathom in Woman." [25]

Earlier in this chapter I suggested not only that *Henry Brocken* traced the growth of the imagination, but that it also examined reality as created by the imagination: specifically, in attempting to recreate familiar characters, de la Mare was examining one more aspect of the life of the mind.

There is no need to disagree with John Freeman's opinion that, "It is an essay upon the eternal theme of the wanderer, a journey backwards through the imaginative kingdom of other writers. . . ." [26] or with Llewellyn Jones who wrote that, in *Henry Brocken*, de la Mare "extends the figures" of a creative work, or, in other words, "tries to get behind them." [27] The theme of the quest reoccurs in all of de la Mare's fiction and in his poetry as well.

But Freeman and Jones did no more than suggest what de la Mare was attempting. It seems obvious to me that de la Mare was testing the validity of the artist's, and more specifically, the writer's imagination. Before Henry Brocken sets out upon his travels he tells of his belief that "somewhere, in immortality serene, dwell they whom so many had spent life in dream of, and writing about." And he continues: "In fact, take it for all in all, what could these authors have been at, if they laboured from dawn to midnight, from laborious midnight to dawn, merely to tell of what never was, and never by any chance could be? It was heaven-clear to me, solitary and a dreamer; let me but gain the key, I would soon unlock that secret garden-door." [28]

The key Brocken discovers is, of course, the imagination. He mounts his steed, gives her free rein, and falls into reverie. When he awakens from it, he finds Lucy Gray, and thus the travels begin. Some reasons for de la Mare's seeming failure to create a convincing child have been examined earlier in this chapter; and, it is hoped, adequate grounds were developed to justify the conclusion that he was not interested in doing so—at least as far as the physical externals are concerned—for he was primarily interested in portraying the mind of a child. This explanation is more tenable in view of the fact that de la Mare professed that in the creation of any character ". . . I am intent, so far as words are capable, on persuading him to appear as real and convincing as I possibly can." [29] He did this as far as his recreations are concerned. That he was not intent on doing so with Henry Brocken is hinted at in the name: a brocken is "an optical phenomenon" and a "specter." [30] If one stands at the rim of a cloud-filled crater with the sun at one's back, one's shadow is projected upon the clouds below, and around the shadow radiates a glowing nimbus. Henry, then, is a projection of the author's mind: a mere shadow, and the vehicle by which de la Mare could absorb, more intently, the reality of the characters who are his primary concern.

De la Mare is reported to have remarked, in reference to writing stories, " 'It is extraordinary how the characters become more real than real people.'" [31] And he maintained that "An imagined 'character' makes his appearance in consciousness no less of his own volition as it were and no less complete than any similar apparition made manifest in a dream." [32]

It is apparent that in coupling an imagined character and an apparition in a dream, de la Mare finds that there is reality in both—imaginative reality, which he felt is the only kind one can be certain of.[33] He did not doubt the validity of apparitions or hallucinations. One particular hallucination he had of a "dwarfish furtive skulking little man" who reminded him of Mr. Hyde impressed him particularly. Commenting years later on this experience he wondered: "Why . . . [he took] the little man in the bedroom for granted? Was it because, being unreal, he did not conflict with reality? Was he more real because he was unreal, or was he more unreal because he was real?" [34]

He thought that living people may be less real than characters in novels, for he maintained that most people believe that a character in fiction is more real than a person dreamed about or an absent friend.[35] He observed: "Who, after all, was the real Fanny Brawne—the girl Keats called a minx, or the girl he adored three weeks later? Was Juliet any less convincing because Shakespeare made her say things that no woman ever says in conversation?" [36]

As de la Mare saw it then, the task of the creative artist was not merely to copy or to piece together bits of his observation, but to distill and essentialize. The artist selects and reshapes and gives new unity to his materials, hoping thus to convey matters of truth and not matters of fact.[37] He felt that: "The creation of characters releases phantasms, so to speak, that may be more potent, elemental, delicate or deadly than any mere man in three dimensions." [38]

That these phantasms can be so created and do inhabit a world more real, perhaps, than what is ordinarily considered to be reality is altogether possible. Not to admit the possibility is to deny all validity of the writer's craft: "The gravity, the earnestness, the intense preoccupation, the artistic conscientiousness involved in the presentation of the scene, situation, characters and so forth of a story or a poem, when they are considered only as so much waking-dream stuff, is indeed little short of ridiculous—if, again, they are that and nothing more. . . . Are they, however, nothing more? Blake's, Coleridge's, Vaughan's world of dreams and of the imagination—is all this nothing, or little more? Can we pass the burden of proof to the world of sensuous actuality?" [39]

As in every other line of speculation de la Mare entertained, he could find no answers. He admitted all possibilities, but that he was on the side of the reality of the imaginative world as opposed to the sensuous is obvious when he suggests: "It may be that, as nature toils arduously to produce a Turner or a Whistler in the real, so humanity mimics the writer of fiction, and discovers a love in being and in fact that it has learned in fiction." [40]

Of course this idea is not original with de la Mare. Among his contemporaries, Joyce Cary was to express this belief in the creative imagination. The artist intuits the truth, or reality, and transforms with the help of creative imagination the mass of raw material that life presents. The more intuitive the artist, the greater will be the truths, Cary believed; and these truths are communicated through his art. Thus, in a very real sense, life copies art; for it is only through art that truth can be known.[41]

William Van O'Connor expresses the views of many contemporary commentators when he writes: "It is hardly an exaggeration to say that we do not know what kind of a world we live in until we have experienced it through the coherent and meaningful configurations of our most original and perceptive artists."[42] Walter Kaufmann discusses this theory in his recent *Critique* and concludes that "the artist does not so much imitate nature as nature subsequently imitates him: he molds the attitudes and behavior of posterity."[43] Kaufmann says, then, that the artist creates what Kant termed a "category." And he goes on to say, using Tristan and Isolde and Mephistopheles as examples: "What makes these creations categories and not merely welcome illustrations is that before Wagner this kind of love, with all its sublimity and bathos, had not been experienced; and Mephistopheles means a new conception of the devil. The great artist is a creator of categories in terms of which posterity understands its own experiences, reinterprets the past, and fashions the future."[44]

This belief is essentially T. S. Eliot's as well: each new work of art alters or reinterprets all past works of art.[45] Perhaps these views are adaptations of Schelling's regard for art as the highest human function, for he believed that, through art, nature, or truth, is revealed; that the creation of the artist serves as a model for humanity to follow.[46] If so, the connection established by Coleridge between the German idealist and English idealism, may be the source of de la Mare's suggestion that "humanity mimics the writer of fiction." Once more, as well, de la Mare is found to be firmly anchored in his times.

[94]

CHAPTER 7

The Three Mulla-Mulgars:
The Moonstone and the Midden

REPUBLISHED in 1919 as *The Three Royal Monkeys*, *The Three Mulla-Mulgars* (1910)[1] was written by de la Mare for the amusement of his children.[2] But there is enough wit and commentary on humanity in this story of the three monkeys who search for the Valley of Tishnar, their ancestral home, to engage the attention of much more sophisticated minds than those of children. And, although deemed "among the most amusing and exciting ever offered to intelligent boys and girls," by Forrest Reid,[3] one questions whether the ordinary child could fully appreciate or be long entranced by the adventures of the three princely monkeys Thimble, Thumb, and Nod, searching for their Uncle Assasimmon's kingdom.

Pointed out by one critic as an exquisite satire[4] and later as an allegory,[5] both of these intentions are discounted by Forrest Reid who states: "I do not believe the author had any other thought than of his monkeys' adventures while he was writing it." [6] It is difficult, however, to accept the latter view, or, indeed, to understand the qualification of the clause, "while he was writing it," particularly in view of de la Mare's own statement:

In all writing, that is, whether in prose or in verse, and whether by intention or otherwise, if we both repeat and listen to the words of which it is composed, two voices are audible and two meanings are inherent—that of the verbal sounds and that of the verbal symbols. Sometimes in open conflict, though never so in fine poetry, usually in a more or less amiable relationship, they may also be in a ravishing harmony; and this in prose no less than in verse; the one clearly evident, the other remaining extremely elusive however closely we scrutinize it, and ultimately, perhaps, beyond analysis.[7]

Two voices are audible in *The Three Mulla-Mulgars;* and it is useless to enquire whether de la Mare intended as much or not. It is apparent that in all of de la Mare's prose fiction there are these two voices—sometimes so much in harmony as to be almost beyond analysis. Forrest Reid admits as much about *The Three Mulla-Mulgars,* and allows the possibility of an allegorical interpretation by concluding: "Still, its beauty relates to the main body of Mr. de la Mare's work: behind earth's loveliness hovers a dream of the absolute: a divine discontent awakens in it and is comforted." [8]

Few other commentators have mentioned *The Three Mulla-Mulgars;* but, in general terms which may be applied to it, G. K. Chesterton suggests that de la Mare utilizes animals as symbols much in the same manner as are employed the beasts in the Book of the Apocalypse; only, he cautions, ". . . they are symbolical in a sense that means something better than the allegorical." [9] It is difficult to ascertain the distinction which Chesterton finds between symbolical-allegorical, and "symbolical in a sense that means something better than the allegorical." There is too much "mystihood" here.[10] One is tempted, therefore, to subscribe, with reservations, to Megroz' conclusion: "The long and perilous journey of the monkeys to a distant Tishnar, their father's homeland, is clearly intended to portray man's journey to a distant heaven, but the allegory, though clear enough, is never intrusive." [11]

Although the word "heaven" is too religious in connotation, the novel is an allegory.[12] But although its primary interest for most adults may lie in the applicability of its theme to the striving of all mankind to capture a dream—to see face-to-face the longed-for inexpressible—its lasting importance to students of de la Mare lies in the fact that it represents once again de la Mare's attempt to find, from yet another point of view, the reality of life. That is to say, by removing himself, as far as was practicable, from the commonplace into the realm of fantasy, the author was able to be more objective in his observations and thus was able to record, imaginatively, what he thought to be truth. In order to do so he created his own mythology, as Edward Wagenknecht has observed, in much the same manner as did William Blake.[13] One does not need a scholar's key, however, to understand de la Mare's symbols because he generally defines each term he introduces.

Paradoxically, while admitting that a mythology was created, Wagenknecht still finds it possible to assert that the novel is not an allegory.[14] The differentiation between allegory and mythology, however, is so tenuous—perhaps mythology is invented for the sake of allegory—that the critic's objections to its being read as an allegory are difficult to entertain seriously. However, one can readily agree with Wagenknecht when he states that the book is not a sermon.

In view of the fact that the author's principal intention was to delight his own and other children, this attempt at classification may seem pedantic pettifoggery. But it will seem less so when one remembers that de la Mare believed that it is the child's imagination that most often perceives or apprehends the truth—and that to children all the world is an allegory. Thus, in writing an allegory, he was confident that what he had to say would be readily understood by his intended audience, if they chose to do so.

W. H. Auden's discussion of allegory is pertinent here and may serve to clarify my position: "The Scylla and Charybdis of Dream Literature are incoherence and mechanical allegory. Without some allegorical scheme of meaning—it is not always necessary that the reader know what it is—the writer has no principle by which to select and organize his material and no defense against his private obsessions; on the other hand, if he allows the allegory to take control so that symbol and things symbolized have a mere one-to-one correspondence, he becomes boring." [15]

De la Mare had to have an "allegorical scheme of meaning" in order to write about three monkeys, in much the same sense that Swift had to in *Gulliver's Travels*, or Charles Kingsley in *Water Babies*, or Lewis Carroll in his Alice tales. Without some such controlling scheme, none of these would have been successful, which success is assured doubly by the fact that there is no "one-to-one correspondence" to be found in them. Some relationships are, of course, to be found between fact and fancy in *The Three Mulla-Mulgars*, and it is in these that the meaning of the allegory can be determined.

The entire world (Munza) in the book is inhabited by Mulgars or monkeys. They correspond to primates; animals are still animals—there are hares and hedgehogs and birds—but the animals can communicate with the Mulgars, of whom there are many species: Mountain-, Laddar- and Fishing-Mulgars, for example. The Mulla-Mulgars are princes of the Blood-Royal because their ancestral home is in the Valley of Tishnar, the realm of the absolute. Man himself is a Mulgar, an Oomgar Mulgar; and although there is just one who figures in the tale—Andy Battle, a shipwrecked sailor—it is obvious that all of the other species of Mulgar fear and hate the Oomgars. Andy, perhaps because he is isolated from other Oomgars, is different, however; he hunts and kills animals merely to stay alive, and he would never shoot a monkey for, as he says, "Andy Battle isn't turned cannibal yet." [16] In fact, when Andy inadvertently captures Nod, the smallest and least practical, yet most powerful of the brothers because he possesses a magic talisman, the man and the monkey become firm friends. "The werry first thing is for me and you to unnerstand one another," he says to Nod; and, talking to each other, they soon learn enough to be able to communicate, after a fashion.

Such love springs between Andy and Nod that, when the occasion arises, the latter saves his human friend from Immanala, who is thus described: "Now, Immanala . . . means, as it were, unstoried, nameless, unknown, darkness, secrecy. All these the word means. Night is Immanala to Munza-Mulgar. So is sorcery. So, too, is the dark journey to death or the Third Sleep. And this *Beast* they name Immanala because it comes of no other beast that is known, has no likeness to any. Child of nothing, wits of all things, ravenous yet hungerless, she lures, lures, and if she die at all, dies alone. . . . And so she is born again to haunt and raven and poison Munza with cruelty and strife." [17]

Immanala alone would argue for an allegorical interpretation of the journey of the three Mulgars; especially so because it is Nod, the least worldly and common-sensical of the Mulgars, who vanquishes her—with the help, it must be remembered, of the moonstone, the magic talisman from Tishnar. Immanala, the "nameless," is the force that preys on all Mulgars in Munza. It is the principle of evil. But, because de la Mare believed evil is absolute,[18] Nod, with the help of the talisman (imagination) overcomes it—just as he has become the friend of Man because he has the imagination to see through externals.

Twice Nod loses the moonstone: once to an emissary of Immanala, and once to a Water-Midden (a handmaiden of Tishnar). In the latter situation, the Midden returns the precious stone to the Mulgar who has given it to her for love's sake. In the former instance, Nod retrieves the talisman by obeying the suggestions given him in a dream, for he knows that dreams are truth and that it is impossible to reach the Valley of Tishnar without the stone. This incident enforces the allegory when one recalls that: "Tishnar is a very ancient word in Munza, and means that which cannot be thought about in words, or told, or expressed. So all the wonderful, secret, and quiet world beyond the Mulgars' lives is Tishnar—wind and stars, too, the sea and the endless unknown. But here it is only the Beautiful One of the Mountains that is meant. So beautiful is she that a Mulgar who dreams even of one of her Maidens, and wakes still in the presence of his dream, can no longer be happy in the company of his kind." [19]

Tishnar, then, may be a place or a thing or even a person—at least in its application to the story of the Mulgars. In the description quoted above, in fact, Tishnar begins to assume the fascinating shape of the "impossible she" which figures so largely in *The Return* although the demands of that novel require that she be a woman. Moreover, it is rare for anyone even to dream of Tishnar and to wake in the presence of that dream: ". . . for very few Mulgars dream beyond the mere forest, as it were; and fewer still keep the memories of their dream when the live-long vision of Munza returns to their waking eyes." [20]

It is now possible to plait the story and the symbols into a consistent allegory. First is the significance of Nod's name: his given name is Ummanodda, while his brother Thumb's is Thumma and Thimble's is Thimbulla. The brothers' names are obviously derived from their given names—they sound homely, pedestrian. But not so Nod's. His name connotes sleep, a light sleep filled, perhaps, with dreams. He was born with mysterious powers which are further enhanced by his possession of the moonstone or imagination without which one could not hope to reach Tishnar, or even, indeed, contemplate the undertaking of the journey.

There is no reason for not believing that the moonstone represents the imagination, for to at least two other writers of dream literature, gems were thought to possess extraordinary significance. Grenville MacDonald speaks of his father's delight in gems: "When held by their beauty, his mind journeyed perhaps into subconscious memories of ancient race-feelings; he was transformed into the pure mystic, his own logical mind becoming subordinate."[21]

In *Lilith,* George MacDonald described as "gleaming like a moonstone," a woman who is also the archetypal Eve.[22] And, when the central character approaches heaven, he observes the gems which adorn its gates: "I saw the prototype of all the gems I had loved on earth—far more beautiful than they, for these were living stones."[23] MacDonald is closely followed in endowing gems with symbolic significance by Charles Williams who introduces the jewels that are to bring destruction to the principals in *Shadows of Ecstasy* in the following manner: "They shone and sparkled; they gleamed and glinted—some set, many unset; stones of every kind revealing the life of stone, colour revealing the power of colour. . . . The man's form seemed to hold in itself depths of mysterious tint . . . disciplined and purged and nourished through many decades by supreme passion."[24]

One further symbol which de la Mare employs makes the allegory even more applicable and also reveals the author's vision. This is the principle opposing Tishnar and different from Immanala, or evil—Noomanossi, who is "darkness, change and the unreturning." The difference between Tishnar and Noomanossi is: "From Tishnar . . . comes the last Sleep—the sleep of all the World. The last sleep of just their own life is Noomanossi. . . ."

One cannot fear Noomanossi, however, for it is not equated with evil. Taking a leopard as an example of the two principles, de la Mare writes: "Her beauty is Tishnar's; the savagery of her claws is Noomanossi's." And he applies this to mankind: "So Munza's [earth's] children are dark or bright, lovely or estranging according as Meermut [phantom of Tishnar] or Nooma prevails in their natures."[25]

The long journey of the Mulgars ends for the reader just short of the Valley of Tishnar. The Mulgars reach the shadows of the mountains wherein Tishnar lies, and as they stop to rest: "Nod turned his head, filled with a sudden weariness and loneliness. In the silence of the beautiful mountains he fell sad, and a little afraid, as do even Oomgar travellers [men] resting awhile in a journey that has no end."[26] And the book ends just as the apprehensive and exhausted brothers see coming out of the valley toward them: ". . . with a band of woven scarlet about his loins, and a basket of honeycombs over his shoulder, a Mulgar of a presence and a strangeness, who was without doubt of the Kingdom of Assasimmon." [27]

The reader is not allowed to enter the Valley where lies the kingdom of their Uncle Assasimmon; in fact, there is reason to doubt that the Mulla-Mulgars will be able to do so, for Nod's feeling of sudden weariness and loneliness and fear as he pauses to rest is compared to man's feeling when "resting awhile in a journey that has no end." There is also an emphasis in the last clause referring to the Mulgar "who was without doubt of the Kingdom . . ." which leads one to believe that the author was trying to convince himself that the three travelers had at last arrived at the Valley of Tishnar.

Nevertheless, although one does not find complete assurance that the odyssey has been successful, insofar as the goal having been reached, it is reasonable to conclude that the journey was a worthwhile one which would have been impossible even to embark upon without the aid of the imagination. Throughout their trip, the Mulla-Mulgars have been abetted, and sometimes hindered, by the other Mulgars they meet. They are respected and helped along, or execrated and deterred, according to the amount of reverence in which Tishnar is held by those they meet. So does it happen to be, one suspects de la Mare is implying, in the world of men. Because Tishnar is "that which cannot be thought about in words, or told, or expressed," and because "it is better to die, going, than to live come-back," [28] the attempt to reach it is all that can be ventured, or recorded, by any man.

CHAPTER 8

The Return:
What Dreams May Come

THE long prose tale, *The Return*,[1] awarded the de Polignac Prize upon its publication in 1910, has since been called everything from a fairy tale to a failure, or ignored—or worse, misinterpreted. Perhaps it cannot be assigned to the same high category of achievement as de la Mare's next novel, *Memoirs of a Midget*: it is less perfectly knit, its language is less poetically rich, its observation of life less perceptive. But in conception *The Return* is hardly less daring. In fact, it is more so; and because it is, when the reader falters, he accuses the author of stumbling. One can easily suspend disbelief and accept the Midget as a credible human being; but it is a different matter to accept *The Return* as more than an echo of the Jekyll-Hyde theme or as a fantastic exploitation of the eternal triangle situation.

But *The Return* is not a horror story, nor merely a story about a man's temporary estrangement from his wife, although a critic as perceptive as J. B. Priestley read it in these contexts and condemned it as being conventional and unrealistic—like "the first novel of a third rate writer." [2] The very machinery of the narrative militates against Priestley's reading. Perhaps it is logical to interpret *The Return* allegorically as does Kenneth Hopkins, and to call it a religious book. Thus, Lawford is Everyman who, in his struggle with Sabathier, has entered the lists against evil, and the novel has religious implications insofar as it proves that "an ordinary weak and rather puzzled man, can enter into a contest with evil—evil backed by all the age-old resources of success in a prospering trade—and still against all odds prevail." [3]

Another interpretation, suggested by Forrest Reid, is that the theme is the reversal of the action in Wordsworth's "Ode on the Intimations of Immortality." Reid writes, "from the shades of his prison-house Lawford moves gradually back, following through storm, gloom and danger a 'visionary gleam' which may be the light of home." [4] And he dismisses any charge that the book is fantastic because of the unusual nature of the incident which precipitates Lawford's struggle: "It is the story of a spiritual upheaval such as might be produced by any violent emotional crisis, religious or otherwise. The actual cause, in comparison with its consequences, is unimportant." [5]

Edward Wagenknecht agrees with Reid's opinion: that de la Mare chose to have Lawford possessed by the spirit of Sabathier is incidental, it is the consequences that matter. "Like a magic talisman," he writes, "Lawford's strange experience tests his life in its every aspect." [6] Earlier R. L. Megroz had viewed *The Return* in essentially the same manner although he protests that the spiritual crisis "pivots upon an occurrence smacking of melodrama." [7]

But, granted that Lawford's transformation is melodramatic, it is neither incidental or gratuitously sensational; it is necessary to the development of de la Mare's theme which is the title of the book—*The Return*. Not only have the commentators ignored the significance of the title, they have failed to explore fully the most important portion of the book: Lawford's relationship to Herbert Herbert and Grisel. True, Reid asks of Grisel, "Is there perchance just the faintest hint that we may identify her with the lost love of Sabathier?" [8] But, because of the implications of this suggestion, he immediately retreats from it: "I do not press the point; I don't know that I want it; for it is certain that the love which springs up between her and Lawford is no memory, no echo of an ancient passion." [9]

It is true their love seems fresh and urgent—it is certainly no warmed-over passion. However, Reid's withdrawal is timely because he was obviously unprepared to explain how Grisel, if she were the love for whom Sabathier committed suicide, could still be alive over a century later. It can be demonstrated, however, that Nicholas Sabathier, eighteenth-century Huguenot suicide, and Arthur Lawford, twentieth-century Englishman, are essentially the same person; that Grisel, beloved by Lawford, is the woman for whom Sabathier died; and that this idea informs the entire novel and leads to an exposition of the author's quest to find outside of man's usual conception of time the ultimate reality of the spirit.

The plot of *The Return* is uncomplicated: Arthur Lawford, an unimaginative, respectable, middle-class Englishman, convalescing from a serious illness, rambles one early autumn day through the cemetery called Widderstone. Musing upon the thoughts of life and death one customarily gives way to in such surroundings, he notices a solitary grave just outside the pale by which he sits. The mottled and worn stone informs him that this is the grave of a suicide Huguenot, one Nicholas Sabathier, "a Stranger to this Parish, who fell by his own Hand on ye Eve of Ste Michael and All Angels. MDCCXXXIX."⁹ Overcome by his unaccustomed exercise and, perhaps, by his thoughts, Lawford dozes on the bench by Sabathier's grave. A short time later he wakes refreshed—so much so that, realizing the lateness of the hour, he runs home, an unaccustomed vitality speeding him along and giving him a heretofore unknown pleasure—an animal feeling of freedom and strength.¹⁰

At home, in his room, still stirring with new life and awareness, Lawford prepares to dress for dinner. Shaving materials in hand, he looks into his mirror. He confronts the face of a stranger: he is not who he was. A physical transformation has taken place which, he soon realizes, echoes throughout his entire being. His face is leaner, almost wolfish, and haunted with an almost desperately longing, sensitive quality; his imagination has begun to stir and he sees beauty and truth in people, objects, and situations that he did not have the vision even to guess at before he went to Widderstone; and he is haunted by voices—whose, he cannot guess—and snatches of memories he cannot identify. Yet, withal, he is essentially the Arthur Lawford that was—the new identity has not superseded, it merely supplements, the old.

Sheila, Lawford's wife, reacts to this situation as would most practical, selfish, insensitive women—her one concern is "What will the neighbors think?" and she cannot help but feel that he is somehow responsible for this thoroughly un-British and, therefore, abnormal occurrence. Her attitude makes it abundantly apparent to Lawford that he cannot rely on her for help in his struggle to find the meaning of this sleight of hand that destiny has played upon him—to overcome it, perhaps; to make the best of it, if necessary.

Thinking that by again sitting at the suicide's grave he may nullify whatever it is that has happened to him, Lawford returns

[104]

to Widderstone, only to find the bench at the grave's edge occupied by a stranger, a man who is singularly uncommunicative until he catches a glimpse in the moonlight of Lawford's face. He introduces himself as Herbert Herbert and invites Lawford to his cottage just beyond the cemetery where later he discloses that Lawford's appearance closely resembles an old print he has of the face of Nicholas Sabathier, the suicide by whose grave Lawford had, on the first visit to Widderstone, fallen asleep. Following this first visit, Lawford becomes a frequent guest at the cottage; and, led by the suggestive and imaginative conversation of Herbert, he speculates unceasingly as to the meaning and reason for the incident that has so remarkably befallen him. At the cottage he meets and also finds himself in love with Herbert's sister, Grisel. Eventually, having plumbed the depths of his own soul, and having examined, with Herbert's help, every possible ramification of his experience, Lawford quits forever the cottage of his friend, Herbert, and his beloved, Grisel, and returns to Sheila and existence.

In his note to Sheila announcing his return, Arthur writes: "I suppose every one comes sooner or later to a time in life when there is nothing else to be done but just shut one's eyes and blunder on. And that's all I can do now; blunder on. . . ." [11]

These words are as poignant as an epitaph to the memory of a prematurely extinguished life and are, in more than a casual sense, just that: they signify Lawford's final and irrevocable turning away from all life other than the dull, daily round of outward appearance. That one must "just shut one's eyes and blunder on" means to Lawford he is closing the inner eye that perceived throughout his harrowing experience the reality of a dream and is returning to the shallow unreality of the so-called life through which he must henceforth, thus sightless, blunder. It is significant, however, that, having written these words, he tears to pieces the letter; for he knows that he can never completely forget that vision of the only reality which he knows he must renounce. He has lived his dream and he can never totally shut his eyes upon it; he has found the "impossible she" and can never banish from his memory the echo of her voice and her last question which brought him to realize that he must return to Sheila: "What peace did he find who couldn't, perhaps, like you, face the last good-bye?"

The Return is not an indifferently successful novel about a bi-

zarre though somewhat hackneyed theme. It is, instead, a searching inquiry into the relationship of the personality or, in religious
terminology, the soul, to the phenomena of life and death, or time
and timelessness. It cannot be gainsaid that de la Mare was preoc-
cupied—almost to the point of obsession one might say if that did
not have the connotation of near fanaticism—with the ultimate
reality. That life and death, sleep and wake, consciousness and
dreams were all of a piece he was convinced, as he was also convinced that "time" is but man's way of ticking off the immeasurable—eternity. Nowhere in his novels is there a clearer statement of
his speculations than in *The Return*. In it he reduces centuries to
the span of days, eradicates the seemingly impenetrable barriers
between life and death, and banishes the differences between
dream and wake. Arthur Lawford's adventure is an account of
man in search of himself; Grisel is the "impossible she" that he
finds. She is the concretion of the inexpressible; the symbol of
mystery, of beauty, of truth, and of peace—the Self—that all men
long to know.

De la Mare could have been thinking of *The Return* in 1918
when he wrote: "The kind and intensity of the love is what is
important in novels—dialogue and story is merely means of dis-
playing them. The greatest of lovers Helen and Paris, for instance,
'as lovers' would bore us in the flesh. We can read about them
pretty nearly *ad infinitum*. For it is always Man, the known, confronted with Woman, the mystery: the impossible she. She is
beauty and memory and strangeness, earth's delight, death's
promise. In a thousand shapes and disguises she visits us." [12]

And again, in 1919, reviewing W. H. Hudson's *The Book of a
Naturalist* for the *Times* when, mentioning the music of the voice
of Rima in *Green Mansions*, he wrote: "The old Adam, the happy
prehistoric child, in every one of us, in response to this incantation
harks back in spirit to the garden of his banishment, wherein Eve
awaits him, and he can be once more happy and at peace, the veil
withdrawn, all old enmities forgiven and forgotten, amid its
beauty and life." [13]

The idea of the "impossible she," already suggested in *Henry
Brocken* and in *The Three Mulla-Mulgars*, is introduced early in
The Return when Herbert Herbert suggests that Lawford has
been possessed by Sabathier: "Supposing—I know it's the most

outrageous theorising—but supposing all these years of sun and
dark, Sabathier's emanation, or whatever you like to call it, horri-
bly restless, by some fatality longing on and on just for life, or
even for the face, the voice, of some 'impossible she' whom he
couldn't get in this muddled world, simply loathing all else; supposing he has been lingering in ambush down beside these poor
old dusty bones that had poured out for him such marrowy hospi-
tality. . . ." [14]

Then, shortly after Herbert has advanced his suggestion and
Lawford meets Grisel, it becomes increasingly evident that she is
his "impossible she." Their meeting also should put to rest any
interpretation of the novel as merely the recounting of a conventional love affair, as J. B. Priestley would have it. It is inconceiva-
ble that Lawford's reaction is that of a conventional philanderer;
for example, when he first meets her "Lawford took a deep
breath, gazing mutely, forlornly, into the lovely untroubled peace
of her eyes, and without the least warning tears swept up into his
own. With an immense effort he turned, and choking back every
sound, beating back every thought, groped his way towards the
square black darkness of the open door." [15]

The reader cannot but ponder the choice of words: why did
Lawford take a deep breath, except that he had been surprised by
her beauty and by his sudden instinctive awareness of the "lovely,
untroubled peace" she promises? From this moment on, it is she
who gives him the courage to do what he feels he must. This effect
is apparent when, after precipitantly leaving the Herbert cottage
upon this first meeting, he finds that he cannot walk past Widderstone Cemetery to return to his home. He stops outside the cottage in a paroxysm of terror. In a moment Grisel is at his side and
hears his confession of fear. At first she implores him to return to
the cottage, "Come back; come back. I am with you, a friend, you
see; come back." It is almost as though she is reluctant to give him
up. She wants him to return with her. But he has the courage to
realize that he cannot: "'I must go on. You see—why, everything
depends on struggling through: the future! But if you only knew
—There!' Again his arm swept out, [he gestures toward the ceme-
tery] and the lean terrified face turned shuddering from the
dark." [16]

It is as though Lawford were afraid of dying; that on his ability

to face existence depends his very life. Grisel realizes immediately
that she cannot coax him back to the cottage and goes instead
with him. Together they go past the cemetery; as they advance, it
seems they are overcoming an oppressive presence. She gives him
the courage that he does not have; and, later, memory of her sus-
tains Lawford when he is again confronted in his home by the
malignant presence that had terrified him in the scene just described. The vision of Grisel persists: the eyes "that seemed to
recall some far-off desolate longing for home and childhood";[17]
and before him there is always "the face of one who seemed pure
dream and fantasy. . . ."[18]

The identification between her and Lawford's "impossible she"
becomes more obvious when Lawford implores her: "Be just the
memory of my mother, the face, the friend I've never seen; the
voice that every dream leaves echoing."[19] In this scene Grisel is
described: "The still grave face beneath the shadow of its veil had
never turned, though the moon poured all her flood of brilliance
upon the dark profile. And once when as if in sudden alarm he
had lifted his head and looked at her, a sudden doubt had assailed
him so instantly that he had half put out his hand to touch her,
and had as quickly withdrawn it, lest her beauty and stillness
should be, even as the moment's fancy had suggested, only a far-
gone memory returned in dream."[20]

Lawford, searching for the meaning of the apparently capri-
cious fate that has not only changed the configuration of his face
but also has etched deeply into his soul, makes, in an internal
monologue, the identification between Grisel and the "impossible
she" even more apparent. "Who was that poor, dark homeless
ghoul, Sabathier?" he asks himself and continues: "Who was this
Helen of an impossible dream? Her face with its strange smile,
her eyes with their still pity and rapt courage had taken hope
away. 'Here's not your rest,' cried one insistent voice; 'she is the
mystery that haunts day and night, past all the changing of the
restless hours. Chance has given you back eyes to see, a heart that
can be broken. Chance and the stirrings of a long-gone life had
torn down the veil age spins so thick and fast.' "[21]

Clearly Grisel becomes an obsession; there is for Arthur Lawford, "one face only before his eyes, the one sure thing, the one
thing unattainable in a world of phantoms."[22] There is no mistak-

ing her identity when we read Lawford's realization during their last moments together: "This, then, was the presence, the grave and lovely over-shadowing dream whose surrender made life a torment, and death the near fold of an immortal, starry veil." [23] Thus, by chance, Lawford has come to know for a little while at least, "beauty and memory and strangeness, earth's delight, death's promise."

The scene in which Lawford and Grisel first meet affords another clue to de la Mare's theme in *The Return.* One sees Lawford as he "groped his way towards the square black darkness of the open door." Indeed, it soon becomes apparent that the Herbert cottage is a symbol of death, the grave which Lawford leaves as Sabathier once left the other grave. It is a peaceful phantasm of a house at the edge of Widderstone which no one admits the existence of and where oblivion can be found. Lawford remarks to Herbert upon his first visit to it: "It's odd, I suppose, but this house affects me much in the same way as Widderstone does." [24] He confesses to having gone by the gate at least twice in the recent past but never having noticed the cottage. Herbert acknowledges: "No, that's the best of it; nobody ever does. We are just buried alive." [25]

The symbol of the tomb constantly occurs in *The Return:* at times it is the Herbert cottage; at others, a cupboard, a drawer, a drawing room. John Atkins' perceptive but brief exploration of the ideas of de la Mare remarks upon the importance of the tomb symbol, and asserts that any enclosed space is likely, in de la Mare, to be the symbol ". . . of all that belongs to the dividing line between life and death," or as de la Mare puts it, "between dream and wake." [26] Atkins advances the thesis that the tomb is one of two poles of de la Mare's "psychological duality. And this duality is the core of, and provides the clue to, all his work." The other pole is "the waste," but unfortunately Atkins does not develop this idea.

The emphasis Atkins places upon de la Mare's preoccupation with the tomb either as the line between life and death, or between dream and wake, is not misplaced. De la Mare testifies to this interest in his work, particularly in *Ding Dong Bell* which is, on the surface, merely a collection of epitaphs.[27] Nor was this interest morbid. As I have pointed out elsewhere, he maintained that it was ". . . as natural to be interested in death as in anything else." [28]

Lawford's wife, Sheila, also serves to reinforce the grave image when she argues that he is somehow to blame for what has happened: " '. . . somewhere in the past, whether of your own life, or of the lives of those who brought you into the world—the world which you pretend so conveniently to despise—somewhere is hidden some miserable secret. God visits all sins. On you has fallen at last the payment. That I believe. You can't run away, any more than a child can run away from the cupboard it has been locked into for a punishment. Who's going to hear you now?' " [29]

Here, in distorted fashion, Sheila summarizes the point of view of the practical, so-called Christian who is fettered with the traditions of a millennia of superstition and stupidity. Nonetheless, she also declares, albeit unimaginatively, the essential theme of *The Return*. The figure of the child locked in a cupboard is surely Lawford locked in the life for which he has no desire. Just as Sabathier cannot altogether quit the cupboard of death, the tomb, so Lawford finds he cannot escape entirely the life he had lived before he had been "Sabathiered." Further, de la Mare's sense of the continuity of the human soul is also expressed in Sheila's declaration that "God visits all sins." It is easy to imagine that de la Mare, while writing this sentiment was thinking that God visits, as well, all virtues.

In *The Return* de la Mare conceives the personality, or soul, or perhaps the essence which is the imagination, as living on through innumerable lives and deaths, searching for the answer to the plaguing mystery. Herbert Herbert illustrates this concept when he first suggests that Lawford has been possessed by Sabathier: " 'I can just conceive it—the amazing struggle in that darkness within a darkness; like some dazed alien bee bursting through the sentinels of a hive; one mad impetuous clutch at victory; then the appalling stirring on the other side; the groping back to a house dismantled, rearranged, not, mind you, disorganized or disintegrated. . . .' " [30]

Reference to the grave is found in the scene where Lawford is again confronted, in his own home, by the same shadowy presence that had terrified him shortly after he had left the Herbert cottage upon meeting Grisel. On the second occasion while the vicar, his old friend Mr. Bethany, waits for him to answer his summons to the door, Lawford struggles down the darkened stairs of the house with ". . . an adversary that, if he should but for one moment close his lids, he felt would master sanity and imagination with its evil." [31] He forces the malignant presence down the stairs into the "airless, empty drawing-room." Then, before the door is closed and locked, he "spat defiance as if in a passion of triumph. . . ." [32] The drawing room is most certainly symbolical of the grave. Lawford has won the second battle with Sabathier, for that is who he thinks the presence is; and this time he has only himself and the memory of Grisel to aid him. He knows now that he will win; for, as he tells Mr. Bethany, "There may be; there is something on the other side. I'll win through to that." But when Bethany, humoring what he thinks is mere fancy, asks just what he means by the "other side," "Lawford hardly heard the question. Before his eyes had suddenly arisen the peace, the friendly unquestioning stillness, the thunderous lullaby old as the grave. 'It's only a fancy. It seemed I could begin again.' " [33] The sudden vision Lawford has is, of course, of the Herbert cottage more silent even than Widderstone, yet engulfed in the thunderous roar of the river Widder—Time. And to begin again is to be born anew.

It is not at all odd to find that a ghost appears in *The Return*. A frequenter of the Herbert cottage, it has been seen there in frantic search for something; then it, or he, disappears, Herbert explains to Lawford, only to return again with a lighted candle in his hand. This description recalls the first meeting of Lawford and Grisel, when as Lawford gropes toward the door, "He caught over his shoulder the glimpse of a curiously distorted vision, a lifted candle, and a still face gazing after him with infinitely grieved eyes. . . ." [34] It also recalls the scene when Lawford forces the malignant presence, Sabathier, down the stairs and locks him in the empty airless drawing room, then leaves a candle which is later found by Sheila.

The fact that Grisel is described as a "curiously distorted vision" with a lighted candle is significant insofar as it suggests that she too, perhaps, possesses some of the qualities of spectral existence. She inhabits, in a sense, both planes of existence, life and death. Further, one cannot fail to see the significance of the ghost's conduct when he reappears with the lighted candle. As Herbert describes him to Lawford, this is what the ghost does: "'He comes, or it comes towards you, first just walking, then with a kind of gradually accelerated slide or glide, and sweeps straight into you,' he tapped his chest, 'me, whoever it may be is here. In a kind of panic, I suppose, to hide, or perhaps simply to get back again.'"

And, when Lawford asks Herbert what he means by this, Herbert replies: "'Be resumed, as it were, via you. You see, I suppose he is compelled to regain his circle, or Purgatory, or Styx, what ever you like to call it, via consciousness. No one present, then no revenant or spook, or astral body or hallucination: what's in a name? And of course even an hallucination is mind-stuff, and on its own, as it were.'" [35]

What de la Mare, in *Behold, This Dreamer!* has to say concerning hallucinations is relevant to this passage in *The Return:* "The experiences of dreaming and waking . . . may . . . occasionally coalesce or overlap; and the half-awakened one may be deluded into accepting the remnants of a dream as real. . . . So, conversely, the mind-stuff of waking life not only persists in dream but by the denizens of dreamland may be likewise dismissed as hallucination." [36]

One can conclude from the evidence that de la Mare is having Herbert suggest that the "mind-stuff" of death persists during periods of wake, of consciousness, or, in other words, of life; and that in either state it may be dismissed as mere hallucination. We have some confirmation of this in Herbert's explanation of the ghost's conduct: "'The poor devil must have some kind of human personality to get back through in order to make his exit from our sphere of consciousness into his. And naturally, of course to make his entrance too. If like a tenuous smoke he can get in, the probability is that he gets out in precisely the same fashion.'" [37]

Here appears to be the suggestion that the ghost is merely another form of consciousness: that to pass from "our sphere of consciousness into his," and vice versa, "some kind of human personality" is necessary. But Lawford wonders why is it necessary that the ghost "be resumed," and Herbert answers: "'Ah, there you have me! One merely surmises just as one's temperament or convictions lean. Grisel says it's some poor derelict soul in search of peace—that the poor beggar wants finally to die, in fact, and can't. Sallie [the Herberts' housekeeper] smells crime. After all, what is every man?' he talked on; 'a horde of ghosts—like a Chinese nest of boxes—oaks that were acorns that were oaks. Death lies behind us, not in front—in our ancestry, back and back. . . .' " 38

That the activities of this ghost present a parallel to what has happened to Lawford is clear. Lawford himself marks the similarity, at which not even the loquacious Herbert scoffs. The fact, further, that Herbert does not venture an opinion as to the reason for the ghost's perambulations but prefers to quote instead Grisel's explanation, and even his housekeeper's, might be considered strange except that it enforces the parallel between Lawford's possession by Sabathier and the ghost's actions even more strongly.

It is pertinent also to consider how closely Herbert's simile, which compares every man to a "Chinese nest of boxes" reflects what de la Mare, in his own person, has to say: "But if the mind, in and by itself, is beyond clear conception, and presumably beyond final self-scrutiny, since watcher will have to watch the watcher and so *ad infinitum,* what of the self, of the soul, of the spirit? The simile of the onion, and of the Chinese nest of boxes at once presents itself, even if definite localization seems absurd." 39

Nor can one scoff at de la Mare's suggestion as to the existence of ghosts; for he asks in an essay: "Can we dismiss with a shrug of the shoulders the belief, long ago propounded by Paracelsus, that we are possessed of an astral or sidereal body, which is usually coincident with the corporate body, but is of a materiality so subtle as to be invisible to the human eye—a body which in sleep or trance or when freed by certain drugs, may depart into the viewless air on errands of its own?" 40

Russell Brain reports that de la Mare seemed not to be interested in the causation or metaphysical status of apparitions; that he "seemed to take them for granted . . . in no way unexpected experiences, to be enjoyed for their own sake"; and that he believed that hallucinations "exist only in one person's private world of perception; and the same might be true of apparitions." 41

De la Mare's use of suggestions from George MacDonald is evident especially regarding the theme of *The Return*. What Lawford longs for is, of course, the return to the Ideal World, which is the only reality. MacDonald's fantasies on this Platonic theme in *Lilith* in particular indicate the impossibility of returning to the Ideal World if the soul is not ready for the ultimate reality. Both MacDonald and de la Mare seemed to feel that to live one must die; but no one can "die" who does not truly long to live; therefore, corporeal death can occur many times for not until the soul is fully prepared can it know the truth. Corporeal life in *The Return* is "life-in-death"—a phrase which shows another connection with Coleridge, incidentally—and Lawford must return to life in death because he is not yet prepared to face the bliss of the true life. De la Mare gives no reason why Lawford should not be: "ripeness is all," as Lear said, and Lawford has not achieved it, just as Mr. Vane in *Lilith* does not. MacDonald held to the hope *The Return* implies, but that de la Mare's last novel was to abandon. It was MacDonald's faith that "To be given a future existence with no memory or touch with the old; to begin again a new life, with new labours and joys and affections, could not be resurrection of the dead, but a new creation having no reference to the old; it would not be a continuation of life, but a cessation; not a new birth, but just a creation of some other soul to take some unknown place." [42]

Again, many of MacDonald's ideas in *Lilith* are paralleled by those in *The Return*. MacDonald questions the reality of our identity—out of our clothes, he asks, who are we? [43] The idea that this world is merely the outer vestment of God is, of course, an old one and can ultimately be traced to Eastern thought; but Carlyle's use of it in *Sartor Resartus* is perhaps the outstanding example in English. Echoing the idea, Herbert Herbert asks, "As for identity or likeness or personality, we have only our neighbors' nod for them, and just a fading memory." [44] And in another context de la Mare ponders the question: "Apart from a certain degree of consent with one's fellow creatures regarding it, [sensuous actuality] that too may, in its own kind, however, be also little more. It is we ourselves who are the only thread on which these beads of experience, bright or dusky, are persistently threaded. For whose trinket box?" [45]

It would seem that, up to this point, I have been mimicking the crime of Pelias' daughters who, in all good faith, dismembered their father and cast his remains into a pot, believing that from it he would rise rejuvenated. Many bits of evidence have been given to substantiate the thesis that *The Return* presents the sum of de la Mare's speculations concerning the relation of human existence or, perhaps, the human personality, to the concept of time. But before all of the evidence is in and I can come to a conclusion, I must review two more scenes from the novel.

In the first of these two scenes Lawford has been staying at the Herbert cottage; the outward manifestations of his experience are disappearing, but what he has learned during those brief few days he can never forget. Yet he realizes that he has not discovered any answers: he has learned to question, "What *is* the reality to this infernal dream?" and he asks Herbert: " 'What on earth *are* we . . . ? Who is it has—has done all this for us—what kind of self? And to what possible end? Is it that the clockwork has been wound and must still jolt on a while with jarring wheels? Will it never run down, do you think?' " [46]

Herbert, for once, in the face of these questions becomes the practical man. He suggests a ten-mile walk for the three of them, after which Lawford, tired, shall sleep soundly at the cottage and awake refreshed. "Then to-morrow, whole and hale, back you shall go; honestly." Herbert refers, of course, to Lawford's home; he seems to promise that Lawford shall return to it. There is a slight reluctance in that afterthought of his "honestly," almost as though a father is reassuring a child. Lawford realizes he must return to his former existence, but he is reluctant; for his experience ". . . makes the old life seem so blank; I did not know what extraordinarily *real* things I was doing without." [47]

Nevertheless, the two men and Grisel go on their walk and have a picnic lunch, after which Herbert naps while Lawford wanders to the crest of the hill from which he gazes idly upon the pastoral scene below of cottages, a farm, a pool of water. While he is thus occupied, ". . . it seemed as if a thin and dark cloud began to be quietly withdrawn from over his eyes. Hill and wailing cry and barn and water faded out. And he was staring as if in an endless stillness at an open window against which the sun was beating in a bristling torrent of gold, while out of the garden beyond came the voice of some evening bird singing with such an unspeakable ecstasy of grief it seemed it must be perched upon the confines of another world." [48]

This vision of Lawford echoes rather pointedly the description

of the ghost who searches the Herbert cottage "questing and nos-
ing no end, and quite methodically too, until he reaches the window." What the ghost sees beyond the window, we are left to
conjecture, but surely the echo of that scene in the present scene is
intentional. We recall that the ghost then "comes back." Lawford
too "comes back" to the Herberts: "He turned unsteadily and
made his way, as if through a thick, drizzling haze, slowly back."
Reaching his companions, he asks menacingly, "What is that—
there?" And Herbert, almost seeming to be feigning surprise, begins to tell Lawford, "The village . . ." only to be thwarted by
Grisel. "Ssh!" she said, catching her brother's sleeve; "that's
Detcham, yes, Detcham." But Lawford is not to be put off by her
reply. " 'No, no; not Detcham. I know it; I know it; but it has gone
out of my mind. Not Detcham; I've been there before; don't look
at me. Horrible, horrible. It takes me back—I can't think. I stood
there, trying, trying; it's all in a blur. Don't ask me—a dream.' " [49]

Grisel then implores him: "Don't think; don't even try. Why
should you: We can't; we *mustn't* go back." To this Lawford replies that he knows it is too late: that Sabathier would know the
meaning of the vision he has seen but that he himself realizes "you
can't go back." One cannot, or should not, return to a former existence, for it would reverse evolution toward the ultimate. He then
pleads with Grisel that she not leave him; and he promises that he
will return to his "earthly home" the following day if she stays
with him for a while now. He implies also that once she did leave
him—but this memory is too vague to articulate—just as he cannot recall the identity of the vision he has had but knows that
Sabathier would recognize it.

Later, back at the Herbert cottage, after a quiet evening of
Grisel playing the piano, and of Herbert reading, Lawford seems
almost at peace with himself. Once again, however, we have an
echo of the ghost in this description of Lawford as he gets up to
go to his room. He "stood up with his candle in his hand and eyed
with a strange fixity brother and sister." Shortly thereafter Lawford retires, after which Herbert and Grisel "turned and looked
long and questioningly into each other's faces": " 'Then you are
not—afraid?' Herbert said quietly. Grisel gazed steadily on, and
almost imperceptibly shook her head. 'You mean?' he questioned
her; but still he had again to read her answer in her eyes. 'Oh,

very well, Grisel,' he said quietly, 'you know best,' and returned once more to his writing." [50]

What Grisel is not afraid of becomes apparent in the second key scene, which immediately follows. It is the day after their walk and Lawford's vision—Grisel clearly and unmistakably ad- mits that she is aware of Sabathier's identification with Lawford. Lawford "whole and hale" after a good night's rest, purportedly, is ready to return home. But he cannot forget the vision. Grisel pleads with him to put it out of his mind: she asks him if there is "the ghost of a reason why you should cast your mind back?"— back to the self that is Sabathier. Lawford answers, "only because I love you." That Grisel is the love of Sabathier, his "impossible she," is further apparent in her halting answer to his confession: "I do—I do love you—mother and woman and friend—from the very moment you came." It becomes even more apparent when she says, "What worlds we've seen together, you and I. And then —another parting." [51] And finally, before they part, they speak to- gether ". . . without question, or sadness, or regret, or reproach; she mocking even at themselves, mocking at this 'change'—'Why, and yet without it, would you ever even have dreamed once a poor fool of a Frenchman went to his restless grave for me—for me?' " [52]

This, then, is Grisel's admission of what she has long known; what she knew, in fact, almost the first moment she saw Lawford a few short days before: she is the love of Sabathier, Lawford is Sabathier. He now implores her to let him stay with her: he calls himself "changeling" and says that he is "converted to Sabathier's God." And he asks her: " 'Think of me as that poor wandering ghost of yours; how easily I could hide away—in your memory; and just wait, wait for you. In time even this wild futile madness too would fade away. Then I could come back. May I try?' " [53]

But Grisel knows that however she may wish for their union, it will not be allowed, because "must is must." At last she explains why she knows it would be futile for him to stay:

"Oh, then, and I know, too, you'd weary of me. I know you, *Mon- sieur Nicholas* [my italics] better than you can ever know yourself, though you *have* risen from your grave. You follow a dream, no voice or face or flesh and blood; and not to do what the one old raven within you cries you *must*, would be in time to hate the very sound of my footsteps. You shall go back, poor turncoat, and face the clearness, the utterly more difficult, bald, and heartless clearness, as together we faced the dark. Life is a little while . . . I know in my heart that to face the worst is your only hope of peace. Should I have staked so much on your finding that, and now throw up the game?" [54]

The old raven, of course, is duty and may be a reference to Mr. Raven in George MacDonald's *Lilith* who is the guide of the hero through the trials he faces. Grisel, with woman's instinctive knowledge, knows that Lawford must face the worst. She resembles Charles Williams' Isabel in *Shadows of Ecstasy* who forces her husband to leave her and seek the ultimate.

Here is the consummate love, the "impossible she" that Sabathier committed suicide to follow in death and then later, through Lawford, burst from the tomb to find in life. There is no doubt in either of their minds that Lawford is, essentially, Sabathier. Grisel has called him such and then later at the cottage she repeats the name to her brother when she says: "Here's Nicholas Sabathier, my dear, come to say good-bye awhile . . ."; and Lawford adds ". . . what I want you to understand is that it *is* Sabathier, the worst he ever was; but also that it is 'good-bye.'" [55] Nor does Herbert reject the identification.

It is Grisel who, to the last, has the courage to face the inevitable separation. Earlier she had suggested to Lawford: "There are dozens and dozens of old stories, you know . . . dozens and dozens, meaning only us." [56] When the moment comes for Lawford to go back to his home, perhaps never to see Grisel again, his resolution fails him and Grisel comforts him: " 'It's only how the day goes; and it has all, my one dear, happened scores and scores of times before—mother and child and friend—and lovers that are all these too, like us. Perhaps it was all before even we could speak—this sorrow came. Take all the hope and all the future: and then may come our chance.' " [57]

Lawford, however, pleads with her: "If we love one another, what is there else to say?"; but Grisel's answer is conclusive, "Nothing, nothing to say, except only good-bye." And then, referring again to Sabathier, she asks, "What peace did *he* find who couldn't, perhaps, like you, face the last good-bye?"

[118]

In this final scene between the two, Lawford is more Sabathier than he is Lawford. Formerly a voice had been urging through his consciousness which he, as Lawford, easily recognized to be Sabathier's. Now, when he protests his love for her, he tells Grisel that "A flat, dull voice keeps saying that I have no right to be telling you all this." It is, without question, the voice of Lawford that reaches through the consciousness of Sabathier; and it is that voice, the "must," that he has to obey. Grisel says nothing more; and as the lovers part: "He touched her hand, peering out of the shadows that seemed to him to be gathering between their faces. He drew her closer and touched her lips with his fingers. Her beauty seemed to his distorted senses to fill earth and sky. This, then, was the presence, the grave and lovely overshadowing dream whose surrender made life a torment, and death the near fold of an immortal, starry veil. She broke from him with a faint cry. And he found himself running and running, just as he had that other night, with death instead of life for inspiration, towards his earthly home." [58]

For all the finality implied in this parting, there is yet a reoccurring suggestion that the separation is not forever. "Take all the hope and all the future: then may come our chance," Grisel had said to Lawford just before he left her. And although de la Mare admitted that there might not be any such phenomenon as chance, he thought that for science so to prove would be the single most revolutionary fact ever discovered.[59] He was surer of himself when he questioned the validity of the concept of time, for he believed that the idea is an artificial one; that each person has a private conception of time; that a "mere series of events" is not time.[60] But, even if it were, he asks, "How much of our experience is verifiable?" [61]

De la Mare also thought that possibly death is merely a state of dreaming; or perhaps that life might more closely resemble a dream and death be an awakening.[62] Thus Lawford's running "with death instead of life for inspiration, towards his earthly home," may be read in the following manner: Lawford, with death (the awakening) for inspiration returns to his earthly home (Sheila) just as Sabathier-Lawford had run from Widderstone a few nights before with life (dream) as his inspiration. Then

Sabathier-Lawford, having found Grisel in the dream of life, must choose death in life as Lawford until his awakening as Sabathier comes.

This interpretation can be clarified somewhat by taking note of the extensive use that de la Mare makes of the "mirror" metaphor, for in none of the other novels does the mirror play such a predominant part.

The mirror has figured extensively in the mythologies of all cultures. All primitive peoples believed that a mirror or other such surface reflected the soul of the person who looked therein.[63] Whether de la Mare was aware of this primitive belief is not important; he did not need to be. Lewis Carroll and Samuel Butler could have provided him with suggestions of the possibilities in mirrors, and so could have George MacDonald in *A Double Story,* and in *Phantastes.* Furthermore, de la Mare was fascinated by mirrors[64] and used the metaphor in several contexts in his non-fiction. For instance, he says that daydreams are "a passive looking-glass-life of active reflections";[65] that as we read a poem, consciousness "becomes a passive mirror of how wide a field of echo and solitude and beauty";[66] and that actuality "preens itself in dream's looking-glass." [67] And he thought that "the mind may be like a mirror, reflecting the outside world. . . ." [68]

In *The Return,* Lawford was first made aware of the change when he looked into a mirror. His reaction is thus described: "He sat there and it seemed to him his body was transparent as glass." [69] Then, after he has been catechized by Sheila and Mr. Bethany, the list of answers which prove that he is Lawford is locked within a little drawer which "lay by chance in the looking-glass." [70] Later a crisis occurs when he begins to doubt his own identity and goes to find the list; he presses "the tiny spring in the looking-glass" and the drawer flies open—empty.[71] Finally, on several occasions, but only when he is in the presence of Sheila or her skeptical friends, his eyes are described as "glassy." [72]

At no time in *The Return* does de la Mare state that the reflection is reality and that what the mirror reflects is not; but it is obvious that he was tinkering with the idea. One recalls Herbert Herbert suggesting, "As for identity or likeness or personality, we have only our neighbours' nod for them, and just a fading memory." [73] Although Lawford has not lost the fading memory, he has lost his own "nod," so to speak; for "he could not, in fact, without the glass before him, tell precisely what the face *was* expressing."[74]

With this evidence at hand, some kind of parallel can be drawn between the ancient superstition and Lawford's case; nor can one reject out of hand a suggestion that de la Mare himself was drawing on some ancient memory common to all mankind in his use of the mirror. For in one instance at least, in a later novel, he intimates that the reflection is the soul.[75]

The metaphor of the mirror and the idea of time, as de la Mare saw it, can be combined in a figure that elucidates the theme of *The Return*. Life, implies de la Mare, is not to be compared to the moment the sparrow knows as he flies through the lighted hall from void to stormy void. Instead, life can be compared to what one sees when standing between two facing mirrors—reflected are image after image after image. In which particular reflection rests the Self, one cannot know. Which of the images is life or death or dream, one does not know; but there is no fixed and impenetrable boundary between the various states. This is not to suggest reincarnation so much as what de la Mare calls a kind of permanent incarnation.[76] Thus it is altogether possible that Lawford and Sabathier are one and the same; as are Grisel and the "impossible she" for whom Sabathier gave his life in an earlier image. As the ubiquitous Herbert Herbert, whose very name suggests redundancy, said, "We know he killed himself, and perhaps lived to regret it after." And Grisel, whose name is an echo of Boccaccio's "patient Griselda," will continue to wait for the image of her loved one to find at last the place where she forever lives. Whether this happy eventuality will occur, de la Mare did not make clear. "The whole question of the relation between the living and the dead—who may not remain dead!—is a difficult one," he confessed some years later.[77] But that the dead may live in the imagination, at least, he was certain: "The dead past may bury its dead, deeper and deeper; yet at the least living thought of them, they will awaken. The dry bones live, they walk again."[78]

CHAPTER 9

Memoirs of a Midget:
The Self Surprised

FOR his startling novel which purports to be the memoirs of a midget,[1] de la Mare employs the familiar device of pretending he is merely the editor of private papers that have been bequeathed to him to dispose of as he thinks best. Thus, as Sir Walter Dadus Pollacke, the editor and friend of Miss Thomasina of Bedlam, known as Miss M. and Midgetina, de la Mare informs the reader in an introduction of the circumstances by which he came into possession of the memoirs, and something of the friendship that had developed between the midget and himself subsequent to the time covered in her memoirs. Sir Walter appears only briefly in the story itself: the midget records that their friendship began through their mutual love for a small statue of the god of sleep, Hypnos.[2] After this significant commencement, their love for and their understanding of each other increase, and Miss M. considers him her firmest friend and most trusted advisor.

Sir Walter writes also that a chance remark of his, unremembered by him, had given Miss M. the impetus to write her memoirs. The remark: "the *truth* about even the least of things—*e.g.*, your Self, Miss M.!—may be a taper in whose beam one may peep at the truth about everything"[3] provides a clue to de la Mare's intentions in writing the memoirs: by seeking to arrive at the truth concerning "the least of things," he hopes to illuminate, at least partially, the truth about all things—all selves.

In order to understand why he chose a midget as a central character, one must discard the notion that the *Memoirs* is "a study of the psychology of the midget. . . ."[4] Miss M. is a midget only in order that the author's point of view may be as far removed from that of the ordinary individual's as possible while at the same time being within the limits of human understanding. Had she been "common sized" the reader's experience would have interfered with his attempt to understand the author's vision. As it is, it is virtually impossible for any reader to identify, physically at least, with the central character. What empathy is engendered, then, between reader and character, is spiritual or psychological; for, although she is vastly different physically from the ordinary person, her point of view is that of any sensitive, perceptive individual.

If this be so, then, one might argue that de la Mare could have created her as any physically normal individual—as an artist, a housewife, a shopgirl, or any other identifiable person—and still have retained her perceptiveness and sensitivity. But to have done so would have restricted the scope of her experience and her vision because of the limitations imposed by the necessity to have ordinary experiences, much more than de la Mare was apparently willing to do. For much the same reason, the central character could not have been a child. Here again, just by creating a more "realistic" character, he would have been hampered by the inevitable limits that childhood would have imposed upon him. And, of course, it is utterly out of the question that he choose the point of view of an animal as he did in *The Three Mulla-Mulgars*. The pathetic fallacy does not enter into a child's appreciation of a story, and *The Three Mulla-Mulgars* was written for children; but adults, for whom he was writing the *Memoirs*, would have been reluctant, if not unable, to suspend disbelief to the extent necessary for complete enjoyment of the *Memoirs* had the central character been an animal, just as for psychological reasons the most aesthetically appealing sculptures are not of animals but of human beings.

It is also possible that the Platonic contempt for the human body is suggested, for the body, as the repository of the senses, receives and communicates to the mind false and contradictory information, thus further obscuring the Ideal World.[5] In writing of a midget, then, de la Mare reduced the likelihood of error in her perceptions of the ideal. Whatever de la Mare's reasons for creating her, however, one must accept Miss M. on her own terms. Belief in her is the something extra, "the additional adjustment" which E. M. Forster finds that writers of fantasy demand of their readers.[6]

A direct source for the midget may have been MacDonald's

Phantastes, in which appears a very tiny woman, an inhabitant of MacDonald's other world, or Fairy-land. Upon being confronted by a young man who is astonished by her diminutiveness, she says, "Form is much, but size is nothing. It is a mere matter of relation." [7] The changes in size Lewis Carroll's Alice undergoes may also have suggested the idea to de la Mare. But in choosing a midget as his central character, de la Mare was undoubtedly influenced by his love for *Gulliver's Travels*. One of his first memories was of receiving for Christmas a copy of Swift's book, and it had since that time always been one of his favorites. [8] Like *Robinson Crusoe* and *Dr. Jekyll and Mr. Hyde,* it was a constant source of inspiration to him. In each of these, the central character is isolated from the main stream of life but particularly in Gulliver's voyage to Brobdingnag one finds a man who, in any ordinary circumstance, would be completely indistinguishable from his fellow men, transported to a society where he is so different as to be a freak. His perceptions are those of an ordinary person, however; and because of them he can see more clearly, without the usual distractions which accompany ordinary circumstances, the follies and excellences of the Brobdingnagians. Furthermore, because he is in most ways similar to his giant hosts, while at the same time being more perceptive of nuances, his comments about them are applicable to his own "normal" country men. The influence of Swift's masterpiece is further enhanced in a scene where Miss M. is at one point transported in a bird cage in much the same manner as Gulliver is by Glumdalclitch.

A difficulty presents itself, however, if we admit the influence of Swift upon de la Mare: because Swift's intention was to criticize contemporary society, it is easy to assume that de la Mare's intention was the same—as do Forrest Reid and others who agree with John Atkins that the *Memoirs* is an "essay into social criticism." [9] Certainly it is possible to see some implications of social criticsm in the novel—indeed, it is difficult to see how any novel which purports to be about people can avoid some social comment—but it becomes increasingly clear that social criticism was not de la Mare's primary intention. Miss M. herself writes: "Nor have I ever, for more than a moment, shared with Lemuel Gulliver his none too nice disgust at the people of Brobdingnag, even at kind-hearted Glumdalclitch. Am I not myself—not one of the quarrelsome 'Fair Folks of the Woods'—but a Yahoo? Gulliver, of course, was purposely made unaccustomed to the gigantic; while I was born and bred, though not to such an extreme, in its midst. And habit is second nature, or, as an old Lyndsey proverb goes, 'There's nowt like eels for eeliness.' " [10]

Furthermore, there is scarcely a reference to any existing institution: the church, the state, industrialism, the structure of society itself—none of these is accorded any but the briefest mention. Perhaps this is one of the reasons why it is difficult to date the action with any success, although the references to carriages, gas lamps, coal-burning trains, and the leisurely pace allow the inference that the period is sometime between 1880 and World War I.

Thus, from internal evidence, it is difficult to see how de la Mare could have intended to write social criticism. If his intentions were to probe society, it was only with an eye to the individuals in it. However, none of the characters, even Mrs. Monnerie, the wealthy collector of oddities, can be taken as representative of a class; and even less can the midget be considered a symbol of the artist, the nonconformist, or Messiah. It is more likely that de la Mare was attempting to discover some part of the truth about the Self; and not only about the Self of Midgetina, for she writes: "Smallest of bubbles I might be, tossing on the great water, but I reflected the universe." [11] She also expresses the opinion in her covering letter that Sir Walter received with the *Memoirs* that ". . . there are not so very many vital differences between 'midgets' and people of the common size; no more, perhaps, than there are between them and 'the Great.' " [12]

It can be concluded, then, that by writing in the first person from the point of view of "the least of things," and by avoiding specific references to actual events and circumstances, de la Mare was able to create an odyssey of a soul in search of itself in the world of no particular time or place. The midget's eye is not a critical one; it is that of an observer—she is the reporter of her spirit's quest for the truth about itself. That the voyage was successful can be concluded from the last recorded statement of Miss M. who, just before her disappearance, tells her housekeeper, "Why, Mrs. Bowater, there's not *room* enough in me for all that's there!" [13]

Except for the first seven chapters, which concern her early years, the chief events of the narrative cover approximately one year in Miss M.'s life—her twentieth. The early chapters are such an effective introduction to Midgetina that the reader has no difficulty in visualizing her: she cannot mount or descend stairs without help; she runs on her father's dresser, trips over his hair brush, and falls, sprawling, beside his watch; she puzzles the family cat, which cannot decide whether to minister to Midgetina as she does to her own kittens. Because she is not often among the common sized, she spends her solitary hours in the woods, becoming friends with caterpillars, spiders, birds, and all of the flowers and other growing things. She also reads fiction and folk tales, but particularly "books of knowledge"; and she assimilates all that she learns from them. Thus, her naturally acute powers of observation are further developed; she admits, "My senses were seven in number, however few my wits." [14]

Some years after the publication of *Memoirs,* de la Mare was to write that Robinson Crusoe possessed seven senses. [15] The analogy between Crusoe and the midget is that they were both isolated from mankind, although of course Crusoe's isolation was more temporal or physical than spiritual. To live in nature, however, de la Mare assumed for him two extra senses. This multiplicity also suggests George MacDonald's belief that "It is only in a seven-fold vision that we get possessed by the Truth in Beauty, and only in like comprehension realize the evil where Beauty is degraded." [16] De la Mare may have borrowed MacDonald's idea, for the midget's seven senses reveal to her more truth than she would have known had she possessed only the usual five. The sixth sense is, of course, intuition. What the seventh is, can only be guessed at, for de la Mare does not say.

The mystery of life and living things haunts Midgetina as much as does the reality of death, and she wonders ". . . how it was that we human beings can bear even to go on living between two such mysteries as the beginning and the end of life." [17] The death of her mother, when Midgetina is eighteen, and that of her father, when she is twenty, force upon her the necessity of trying to find the answers to her questions elsewhere than her family home in Kent. It is arranged that she go to Beechwood, a village some miles from London, to lodge with Mrs. Bowater, who is "rather a faithful feature of the landscape than a fellow being" but who nevertheless becomes a firm friend.

Not many weeks after her arrival at Beechwood, where Midgetina continues her solitary pastimes of reading and taking long solitary walks about the countryside, Fanny, Mrs. Bowater's schoolmistress daughter, returns home for the holidays. Now, Miss Thomasina's adventure begins. She plumbs for the first time the depths of passion and despair, for she becomes enraptured with the beautiful, though willfully cruel, Fanny, who, used to such veneration, either ignores or unmercifully teases her. One feels, however, a sense of identification between the two women who are similar only in that they are both beautiful. Fanny is the woman of the world who acknowledges that "Facts are facts; and I'm not sorry for them, good or bad";[18] and who maintains, "I can't and won't see things but with my reason." [19] Fanny's world, too, is entirely different from the midget's: "It is neither dream nor nightmare, Midgetina, but wide, wide awake." [20] At least one critic has categorized the relationship between the two women as a homosexual one; [21] but the argument has little validity because of de la Mare's opinions of Freudian psychology. It is sufficient to say here that, although he never minimized the importance of sex, he was not content to explain human beings merely in terms of it.[22] Furthermore, to call the midget's infatuation with Fanny homosexual is to ignore the fact that in all of de la Mare's novels the love relationship is the reaching out of one soul to another: that Midgetina could never touch Fanny's soul or Self was her tragedy, just as later in the novel Mr. Anon's failure to reach hers is his tragedy.

The friendship of Midgetina and Fanny begins at Fanny's suggestion when one night they are watching the stars and she says, "We are going to be great friends, aren't we? . . . Would you like that?" The midget agrees but with some reservation: "But I must come to you. You can't come to me. No one has; except, perhaps, my mother—a little." [23] Under the ineluctable scrutiny of the silent stars, the two women establish their identities; it soon becomes obvious which of them is the most real in de la Mare's terms. The midget tells Fanny: "If I went away, you couldn't follow. When you go away, you cannot escape from me. I can go back—and *be* where I was." And Fanny replies, "If . . . I could care like that too, yet wanted nothing, then I should be free too." [24]

The meaning of these speeches is unmistakable. The midget is free because she has imagination, which Fanny lacks; she can come and go as she pleases in her self—past and present and future. Therefore, she has some degree of self-realization.[25] Fanny is too much in the world, too much a part of it; she longs for love but she will never know it because she is too ambitious for the things of the world. She loathes people; and, in an indictment of them, she reveals the difference between herself and the midget: "The snobs they are! I have soaked in it for years . . . you suppose that all that matters is what you think of other people. But to be perfectly frank, you are out of the running, my dear. I have to get my own living, and all that matters is not what I think of other people but what other people think of me." [26]

Here is another realistic, unimaginative woman, very similar to Sheila Lawford in *The Return:* the antithesis of everything in which de la Mare believed. The midget knows Fanny for what she is; she asks herself: "If we are all shut up in our bodies as the poets and the Scriptures say we are, then how is it that many of the loveliest seem to be all but uninhabited, or to harbour such dingy tenants; while quite plain faces may throng with animated ghosts?" [27]

Fanny's beautiful body is inhabited at best by "dingy tenants," and it is obvious that there can be no bridging of the gap between Midgetina and Fanny. Midgetina could never understand a person capable of saying as Fanny does: "Do you really suppose that to be loved is a new experience for me; that I'm not smeared with it wherever I go; that I care a snap of my fingers whether I'm loved or not; that I couldn't win through without that? . . . Isn't half the world kicking down the faces of those beneath them on the ladder? I have had to fight for a place." [28]

The midget pleads with Fanny to be a little more charitable and offers to help her, saying: "Oh, Fanny do listen to yourself, to what you are." Fanny rebuffs her with a horrifying denunciation:

Thank you: and I'd rather suffocate than accept your help—now. Listen to myself, indeed! That's just the pious hypocrite all over. . . .

[128]

I tell you, Midgetina, I hate you: I can't endure the sight or sound or creep or thought of you any longer. Why? Because of your unspeakable masquerade. You play the pygmy; pygmy you are: carried about, cosseted, smirked at, fattened on nightingales' tongues. . . . But where have you come from? What are you in your past—in your mind? I ask you that: a thing more everywhere, more thief-like, more detestable than a conscience. Look at me, as we sit here now. *I* am the monstrosity. You see it, you think it, you hate even to touch me. From the first moment to last you have secretly despised me—me! I'm not accusing you. You weren't your own maker. As often as not you don't know what you are saying. You are just an automaton. But these last nights I have lain awake and thought of it all. It came on me as if my life had been nothing but a filthy, aimless nightmare; and chiefly because of you. . . . Did I make myself what I am, *ask* to be born? No, it's all a devilish plot. And I say this, that while things are as they are, and this life is life, and this world my world, I refuse to be watched and taunted and goaded and defamed. . . . Listen, I say. Come out of that trance! I loathe you, you holy imp. You haunt me.[29]

When it is apparent that Midgetina cannot reply, Fanny says: "Perhaps you didn't quite hear all that, Midgetina. You led me on. You force things out of me till I am sick. But some day, when you are as desperate as I have been, it will come back to you. Then you'll know what it is to be human. But there can't be any misunderstanding left now, can there?" [30]

And the midget answers: "No, Fanny. I shall know you hate me." Fanny then asks, "And I am free?" And, although Miss M. nods assent, she does not fully understand Fanny's question. One recalls that early in their relationship, Fanny had remarked that, if she could love as did Midgetina and want nothing, then she would be free.[31] Now it is apparent that Fanny cannot love, and ever her hate seems not to be motivated by anything but fear and self-hate. Here the identification between the two women seems strongest: Fanny is material, the midget is spiritual. But the body refuses to recognize the imagination for what it is, or perhaps it cannot. When Fanny accuses the midget of being "a thing more everywhere, more thief-like, more detestable than a conscience," she is really looking into her own soul; and, in accusing the midget of making her own life "nothing but a filthy, aimless nightmare," she is recognizing her own inability to come to terms with herself.

It has been suggested that Fanny is an incarnation of evil;[32] but,

[129]

although it is true that de la Mare often expressed a feeling of the presence of evil,[33] one cannot accept Fanny as an incarnation of evil because it is difficult to do other than pity her. One is inclined to accept Midgetina's summation: "To my lonely spirit she was a dream that remained a dream in spite of its intensifying resemblance to a nightmare." [34]

Mr. Anon is in many ways the masculine counterpart of Fanny; he is bitter, cynical, a hater of mankind: "Human beings are no better than sheep, though they don't always see the dogs and shepherds that drive them," [35] he maintains. He cautions Miss M. not "to fall into their ways and follow their opinions" for that would be to lose her Self.[36] But he cannot turn her away from her interest in and love of people.

That Mr. Anon, another creature of approximately the same size as Miss M., should live in the same neighborhood may seem to be a most fortuitious coincidence, but, as Miss M. explains, "Yet, after all, whales are but little creatures by comparison with the ocean in which they roam, and the glow-worm will keep tryst with glow-worm in forests black as night." [37]

And also that this ugly, deformed dwarf should have a beautiful soul and no name but Mr. Anon, which is given him by Miss M., is not astonishing for, as she explains when discussing her own name, "Some one I know always calls me Midgetina, or Miss Midge, anything of that sort. I don't mean . . . that it doesn't *matter* what we are called. Why, if that were so, there wouldn't be any Society at all, would there? We should all be—well—anonymous. . . . Not that that makes much difference to good poetry." [38]

There is more than a hint in this passage of Alice's conversation with the gnat in *Through the Looking Glass*. When the gnat asks what is the use of giving names to insects if they do not answer to them, Alice replies: "No use to *them* . . . but it's useful to the people that name them I suppose. If not why do things have names at all?" To which the very sensible gnat replies, "I can't say." [39] Mr. Anon(ymous) then has no use for a name; he is simply there. He may be a dream symbol. And in physical appearance at least, there is in him a suggestion of Mr. Hyde, a character to whom de la Mare often referred.[40] The implication that Miss M.

and Mr. Anon are eventually reunited after his death suggests that she had finally learned that outer appearances—his repulsive form —mean absolutely nothing. She does not, until then, perceive the Dr. Jekyll beneath his outer ugliness. During his life she was unable to accept his love, for she had not learned that truth. In fact, when he declares his love for her, she is revolted and tells him never to say again what he has told her. She does, however, offer him some compensations: "Even if I cannot love you, you are part of all this [life]. You feed my very self. Mayn't that be enough?" [41] And she also tells him, "I share my secretest thoughts—my imagination, with you; isn't that a kind of love?" [42]

Thus an uneasy compromise is made between them: Miss M. brings some little joy to Mr. Anon although he does not think that his love for her will ever be requited. The final irony of their relationship occurs, however, when Mr. Anon, unable to share her all-pervasive curiosity about every facet of existence, within and without, and revolted by her decision to display herself at a traveling circus, sacrifices his life to preserve his idea of her. Just before he dies, the midget, unaware of his fate, believes that at last they will be able to live at peace together and with mutual understanding.

In a postscript to the *Memoirs,* Miss M. admits her reminiscences have been painful to write because in doing so she has relived the many experiences of the "wildest, happiest, cruellest, dearest, blackest twelve-month" of her life. Still she finds that writing them has been worthwhile, for:

> Even when most contemptuous and ashamed of myself, I have still found comfort in the belief that truth is a wholesome medicine, though in essence it may be humanly unattainable. And my work has taught me this too—not to fret so foolishly as once I did, at being small and insignificant in body; to fear a great deal more remaining pygmy-minded and pygmy-spirited. . . . We *cannot* see ourselves as others see us, but that is no excuse for not wearing spectacles; and even up here, in my peaceful lonely old Stonecote, I must beware of a mind swept and garnished. Moreover my hour must come again: and his. [43]

This passage may serve to indicate how very real Miss M. is: her size is merely a convenient device. As de la Mare reveals more and more of her Self, her size becomes less and less important;

and, except for the occasional references to it and the one or two unusual circumstances of her life, such as when she exhibits herself in the circus, the reader is inclined to forget all about her physical abnormality. In other words, on the literal level she epitomizes any acutely perceptive, frank, and imaginative individual. She seeks the truth, but the knowledge that it may not be attainable in this life does not daunt her. Outward appearances mean little to her, for she realizes the mind and the spirit are the important things. She feels the isolation to which all human beings are condemned, but she expresses faith that at last it will be mitigated. In this last, she is not to be disappointed.

That her hour does come, and that Mr. Anon had something to do with it, Sir Walter's introduction intimates; for he reports that, some time after the *Memoirs* had been completed, Miss M. disappeared from her home, Stonecote, under most unusual circumstances. Sir Walter records that Mrs. Bowater, the housekeeper, informed him that on the evening of her disappearance she had heard a stranger's voice talking with Miss M. Being the only person who could admit anyone to the house, Mrs. Bowater had been somewhat perplexed and shortly went to investigate. There was no one in Miss M.'s apartment; only a garden hat and a cape were missing from the wardrobe; and a note pinned to the carpet read, "I have been called away.—M." A protracted search by Sir Walter revealed no clues to the midget's disappearance. He concludes: "Nor is it to be assumed that some 'inward' voice—her own frequent term—had summoned her away; for Mrs. Bowater immovably maintains that its tones reached her ear. . . ." [44] One can but surmise that the voice was that of Mr. Anon, and that he had come to take her where she so longed to go—her spiritual home. This supposition is enhanced when one recalls that his last word to her while living was: "Wait"; and remembers also her earlier confession: "I can never, never love him; but he shall take me away—away—away. Oh, how I have wasted my days, sick for home."

This novel, the most carefully wrought of de la Mare's prose works, is in many ways the most difficult to interpret. That the literal level of meaning cannot be seriously intended as the sole one is obvious to the most casual reader. That it is not an allegorical account of the problems of the individual or of the artist in the world of commonplace is obvious for reasons presented earlier in this chapter.

It can be suggested that the *Memoirs* is an examination of three aspects of the human condition: the heart, the intellect, and the spirit. In this reading, Mr. Anon is the heart; Fanny, the intellect; and Miss M., the spirit or the imagination which, although touching on the other aspects, according to de la Mare's view, imperfectly understands them, at least in this life.

There is much justification for this reading: Fanny is the practical, coldly rational intellect. Because she is such, she cannot be reached by Miss M.'s intuitive, spiritual love. According to her infinitesimal friend, Fanny hides "in her own outside." Fanny always turns a deaf ear to her "inward voice" and even to Midgetina's pleas: "Oh, Fanny, do listen to yourself, to what you are." [45] Fanny, moreover, will never know the midget for what she is; she can only see outer appearances and she does not share the midget's point of view, as she reminds the midget, ". . . you must remember, dear Midgetina, that you will never, never be able to see things in a truly human perspective." [46] What Fanny thinks the "human perspective" is, we were reminded when she says: ". . . all that matters is not what I think of people but what other people think of me." [47]

It is not too impossible to conceive of Mr. Anon as a representation of love—the heart. However, it is a love that attempts to justify itself and is, therefore, selfish; his very death is an indication of his possessiveness. The thought cannot be dismissed that possibly he loves Miss M. principally because she is the only other person he has met who is of comparable size. Furthermore, because he never makes his peace in a world of Brobdingnagians— he hates them all, and even mistrusts the kind Mrs. Bowater—he can never really touch, except momentarily, Miss M.'s essential being; for she maintains of the very people he hates: ". . . I tell you I love them. They are my own people; and I'd die for them if they would only forget what's between us and—and share it all." Nevertheless, Mr. Anon is the stranger in a world of strangers who comes closest to speaking to Miss M. self to self: ". . . I am, as you might say, in my own *mind* with him. I think he knows a little what I am, in myself I mean," she writes. Thus, we must accept her testimony in evaluating him.

For designating the midget as the "spirit," one can find much evidence; but only, however, if one accepts the identification of spirit with imagination—that is to say, without religious connotations. Certainly, she is more nearly her Self than Fanny could ever be her own Self. Then, too, she has the imagination that can love almost without reservation—a quality Mr. Anon does not possess. Of this capacity, she writes: "If a small heart can fall in love with the whole world, that heart was mine. But the very intensity of this greed and delight—and the tiniest shell or pebble on the beach seemed to be all but exploding with it—was a very severe test of my strength." [48]

Nevertheless, she is capable of comprehending the horror of the world, as is attested in her recollection of a childhood experience:

As one morning I brushed past a bush of lads' love (or maidens' ruin, as some call it), its fragrance sweeping me from top to toe, I stumbled on the carcass of a young mole. Curiosity vanquished the first gulp of horror. Holding my breath, with a stick I slowly edged it up in the dust and surveyed the white heaving nest of maggots in its belly with a peculiar and absorbed recognition. "Ah, ha!" a voice cried within me, "so this is what is in wait; this is how things are"; and I stooped with lips drawn back over my teeth to examine the stinking mystery more closely. That was a lesson I have never unlearned. [49]

As the foregoing passage attests, the midget has powers of observation developed to an uncommon degree, and she does not shy away from the unpleasant. A paradoxical statement of hers, ". . . a thing *is* its looks, if only you look long enough" would seem to indicate that she lives, as does Fanny, "on the outside." However, her ability to "look" at things is the ability to attend to their essence, for, as de la Mare wrote:

Attention is not only a focusing of the senses, the mind, and the spirit; it is the half-conscious surrender of all one's past to the object scrutinized. As we attend, instantaneously, we dye, dilute, distill, essentialize, compare, and so remake. Even the absorption of a child has more facets of vision than a fly; its ancestry gazes out from beneath its brows. As we grow older, so more and more of our experience of life transmutes what is present. Out of our paradise we look upon the face we love; and beast or devil is lurking somewhere in the burning or destructive stare of desire or envy. [50]

The last sentence of this selection is another clue to the difference between the midget and Fanny. From her "paradise" the midget sees Fanny as "just a beautiful body—with that sometimes awful Someone looking out of its windows." [51] The Someone in Fanny looks upon the world with the "destructive stare of desire or envy," for Fanny has learned this lesson from attending to the world: "Take all: give nothing. There's no other means of grace in a world like this." [52] A lesson taught by desire and envy, it brings about her own spiritual destruction. She has not learned, as the midget has, that

All things stale and lose their virtue, the best and the worst, the simple and complicated, the plain and beautiful, impulse as well as artifice, unless we attend to them; give to them at least as they can bestow. Not that a forced ardour can restore the tinge of strangeness to the familiar which at least once in life was the secret of its charm. Yet it would never be a loss to ponder an instant on the colours of an apple before we peel it; or on the exquisite green-bronze iridescence of a starling's plumage before we dismiss its owner as a pest. No hunter surely, not even Nimrod himself—unless, like Othello, the pitiable prey of jealousy—could kill any creature at the very moment when he was spell-bound with admiration of its beauty, and therefore of its mystery.[53]

The midget, as spirit, or the essence which is the imagination, has also learned that "All beauty—and in spite of the horrors of life, in spite of the fleetingness of happiness, man has made this supreme discovery—appeals to our delight in mystery and wonder." [54]

One can be sure that she will never lose her delight in beauty and the sense of mystery and wonder. It is through these capacities and "with the aid of a feeble taper, introspection," [55] that Miss M. is able to discover at least the partial truth about her Self, and thus, with the publication of her *Memoirs*, to illuminate, again partially, all Selves. It is to this task that Walter de la Mare committed himself in undertaking to write *Memoirs of a Midget*. The meaning he extracts from the midget's odyssey is, in a sense, melancholy: one's Self can never really find or be at peace with another Self, at least in life. The brief moment of union that Miss M. experiences with Mr. Anon underscores the irony:

He knelt beside me, held out his hand as if to touch me, withdrew it again. All presence of him distanced and vanished away in that small darkness. I prayed not to think any more, not to be exiled again into—how can I explain my meaning except by saying—Myself? Would some further world have withdrawn its veils and have let me in then and for ever if that lightless quiet could have continued a little longer? Is it the experience of every human being seemingly to trespass at times so close upon the confines of existence as that?

It was his own harsh voice that broke the spell.[56]

Nevertheless, exile through the Self must always be, except for such brief encounters, by living "in a world of the imagination which is in everlasting relation to its heavens," the Self not only endures but emerges triumphant, although exactly how or when we are left to conjecture because de la Mare himself was not explicit about the final fate of Miss M. With a dash of humor as well as truth, she says at one point: "Oh dear, how simple things are if only you leave them unexplained." [57] Her memoirs do not, cannot, explain: "All that I write, then, is an attempt only to tell, not to explain. I realize that sometimes I was pretending things, yet did not know what I was pretending; that often I acted with no more conscience or consciousness, maybe, than has a carrion crow that picks out the eyes of a lamb, or a flower that draws in its petals at noon." [58]

But the final triumph of Self-knowledge comes immediately thereafter: "Yet I know—know absolutely, that I was, and am, responsible not only for myself, but for everything. For my whole world." [59] And perhaps the meaning of the whole Self is revealed in the last paragraph of the *Memoirs*: ". . . of this I am certain; that it will be impossible to free myself, to escape from this world, unless in peace and amity I can take every shred of it, every friend and every enemy, all that these eyes have seen, these senses discovered with me. I *know* that." [60]

CHAPTER 10

At First Sight:
The Journey Ends

Whatever preparation in the body and mind, unperceived by ourselves, has been made for its reception, Love waits for no man. He neither knocks nor is announced. We "fall" in love, and in so doing soar, for the time being at least, into an earthly paradise. . . . In a moment we have staked our one and only bright penny and have lost; and in so doing have won a hitherto unrealised self. . . .

"At first sight" is the well-worn phrase, and sight is the most delicate, though not the most immediate, of the senses. But how is it possible that consequences so extreme can come of so casual a cause? Clearly they can't.[1]

WALTER DE LA MARE's last attempt in the novel form investigates the phenomenon of "falling" in love "at first sight." In a sense, also, *At First Sight* [2] is almost a précis of *The Return;* a distillation of that early novel, as it were, which eliminates all of the supernatural machinery and explorations of time and reality: all that remains is a recreation of the brief rapture Lawford knew in coming face-to-face with the "impossible she." Arthur Lawford's realization that the mystery is impossible to know, except momentarily, in this life is underlined in the tragic outcome of Cecil Jennings' experience in *At First Sight.* In *The Return,* however, there was implied some hope that the temporarily known would be at last completely known somewhere, sometime. *At First Sight* offers no such solace.

There is also a similarity between this novel and de la Mare's masterpiece—*Memoirs of a Midget;* for here the point of view of the central character is as unusual, perhaps even more so, as the midget's. But it is not a voyage of discovery into the Self to the extent recorded in the *Memoirs.* Cecil Jennings in all respects but one is an apparently normal young man leading a quiet, sheltered life—somewhat of a dandy, with a modest income. In appearance he differs little from other young men except that he wears a green silk eye-shade because of a peculiar ocular disease.

When this protective shade is introduced, the reader is immediately reminded of Hawthorne's story, "The Minister's Black Veil." [3] But the similarity ends here—the minister's veil functions to remind his parishioners and himself of the sin which lies within; Jennings' eye-shade, on the other hand, does not. It serves on the literal level a practical function: it protects his eyes which, from birth, have been incapable of looking up. This fact known, one might assume that de la Mare was symbolizing the impoverishment of the soul of the young man who could not "look up," so to speak, spiritually. But this reading must be rejected also because of the excruciatingly ironical portrait of Canon Bagshot who, persuaded that Jennings would be able to perform the feat physically if only he learned to do so spiritually, catechizes the young boy mercilessly in matters of the spirit. After one such fruitless attempt, Bagshot concludes: "But though it is your lot in life to be compelled to be unable to face the world boldly, as Christian faced Apollyon, in *spirit* you can, like all of us, at least learn to look up. And I, as one of the humblest of spiritual pastors and masters, if you remain recalcitrant, must find some means of insisting upon your making the attempt." [4]

Bagshot, the "humblest of spiritual pastors," obviously does not speak for the author: the idea of "looking up" spiritually is never advanced by de la Mare except in such ironic terms. It is the idea of "looking in" that interests de la Mare, and this is what Cecil's eye-shade should force him to do. At the same time, however, it is not revealed to the reader, at least until the young man falls in love, precisely what Cecil sees; one is aware only of the dull, daily round of his outward existence. And it becomes evident after he meets Miss Simcox that his inner knowledge is not enough.

Cecil grows to manhood living with a grandmother who is as unimaginative as Sheila Lawford and Fanny Bowater, but who is an infinitely more malevolent person. Mrs. le Mercier is the epitome of possessiveness: "She could be liberal, even magnanimous to any one really dependent on her, and she never humiliated the humble." [5] And although she is apparently unrelenting in her efforts to secure the services of specialists for her grandson, she steadfastly opposes taking the steps that they recommend as possible cures for his condition. De la Mare's mastery of portraiture again creates a prototype of all those who cannot love and who, therefore, can never know, even momentarily, what life is. Cecil comes early to terms with her: "And partly because he could not help himself and partly because of a natural indolence, he had just gone his own way—the way within, that is—without saying very much about it and without deliberately setting his will against hers." [6] This, then, is Cecil's existence: tea every afternoon, a daily walk, sleep—fenced in by routine, his outward vision circumscribed, and his inner life somnolent.

Then out walking one day, he sees a glove, just dropped, which he retrieves. A change in him occurs: something has happened to break the routine. For the ensuing few days he haunts the street where he found the glove looking for the young woman to whom it belongs. He does find her; that is to say, they find each other in an electric moment of recognition: "It was a wilderness that had begun to blossom like the rose. They had discovered the solitude only two can share." [7] In a word, Cecil and Miss Simcox have, at first sight, "fallen" in love. Each is the other's longed-for stranger. Cecil echoes her confession: " 'In the whole of my life I have never talked to any one like you. I mean that *I* have never really talked before to any one. . . .' " by saying: " 'I *am* you. You are here.' " [8]

The power of their love enables Cecil to see things he has never seen before: " 'The moment you come, my mind is like another place. I have never seen anything of this before—this green, this loveliness, that water. I don't even know what they are; they have gone back to their own secrets, as, do you remember—when you were a child?' " [9] But for diverse reasons, shortly after Cecil and Miss Simcox have found each other, the two lovers must part— she, to death in the river; he, to death in life; but not before, however, Cecil has managed the heretofore impossible: he looks, despite the most agonizing physical torture, into her face—and "found himself gazing eye to eye with this phantom of his dreams." [10]

Their separation is inevitable, although it is not dictated by practical or material circumstances. Cecil and his dream separate for the same reason that Grisel and Arthur Lawford in *The Return* must, as a comparison of their final moments together indicates.

To Lawford's question, "If we love one another, what else is there to say?" Grisel's answer is simply: "Nothing, nothing to say, except only good-bye." [11] In *At First Sight* Cecil's loved one says to him: "I love you. . . . And simply because of that, it must be— we must leave each other here." [12]

Precisely because lovers find "an earthly paradise," and win "a hitherto unrealized self" they must part; for in de la Mare's world fully to apprehend the mystery and secret of life is impossible. Whether it shall ever be possible except in moments of indifferent duration, he does not say. But, because Cecil had only begun to "see," his vision was momentary. In *The Return* Sabathier as Lawford returns to his Grisel; and, although their earthly union is brief, it is implied that a more lasting reunion is possible in death. In the *Memoirs of a Midget,* Mr. Anon's love for Miss M. is not reciprocated until too late; but Mr. Anon's eventual return to the midget and their lasting reunion is unmistakably implied. However, the final paragraph of *At First Sight,* implies a different fate for Cecil after his beloved leaves him: "The sun was riding high in the heavens next morning, and the scene around Cecil alive with its scintillating summer beauty—skylarks in the empty blue, butterflies wavering from flower to flower, the blossoming waters radiant with light—when, too much worn out with pain and hopelessness to pay any attention to such elusive and illusory promises, he realized at last that she was gone never to return, and he groped his way back to [grandmother] and his life." [13]

"Never to return." The finality of these words admits of no hope that the lovers shall ever be reunited. Thus the irony of the title is underscored, for in the first sight is inherent the last. Why this should be so, de la Mare cannot explain. "To realize and to communicate" [14] is what love seeks to do. It effects, in a sense, a "conversion of the mind";[15] and however fallible or short lived or bitter its consequences, it is the transcendent blessing of life.[16] *At First Sight,* then, is a brief record of Self discovering Self; but Cecil has not the knowledge of Self that Miss M. was able to acquire; and a brief perception of the ideal is not enough to sustain him in the Ideal. The entire experience may as well have been a dream; but, as dreams are only fragments of reality, they cannot endure.

CHAPTER 11

A Final Estimate

WALTER DE LA MARE's novels suggest that the imagination is unable, in this existence at least, to comprehend the mystery of life; to apprehend, to be aware of its beauty and strangeness, is all the imagination can hope to do. Yet, no matter how briefly, it is in the imagination that we truly live.

The novels show that de la Mare was not a follower of any particular philosophy, but that in his easy eclecticism he came closest to the Idealists, either borrowing from or paralleling the speculations or methods of Plato, Schelling, Coleridge, Blake, Lewis Carroll, and George MacDonald, among others. The one attribute de la Mare held in common with all of them was a fundamental belief in the imagination. A point of difference with some of them was that he did not attempt to construct a system. Nor did he possess, apparently, the religious faith that led George MacDonald, for one, to believe that he had found at least a partial explanation of the inscrutable mystery.

These two qualities—they cannot be called failures—may be among the reasons for de la Mare's having abandoned the novel form and for his concentrating instead on the short story, the poem, and the anthology. On the one hand, a novel must be structured to present a sustained and developing vision: "spots of time" cannot be developed into a coherent novel. The short story and the poem are forms in which a brief vision can be more effectively presented. That is to say, his vision after *Memoirs of a Midget* was not one that could be sustained in a longer medium: perhaps that is why *At First Sight,* his last attempt in the novel, is essentially a short story.

Then, on the other hand, de la Mare's anthologies *Early One Morning* (1935), *Behold, This Dreamer!* (1939), and *Love* (1943), are evidences of a man seeking the answers in the art of other men. It is impossible to indicate the scope of his search: it was unremitting. His arrangement of the selections indicates that he was creating something new, and the introductions to the volumes are as wise and as witty as one could wish. The anthologies well merit the epithet, "creative."

An even more unusual work, and one which again reveals a search for truth, is *Desert Islands and Robinson Crusoe* (1930). In this compendium of travel literature, the footnotes exceed in bulk the text, reminding one of Lowes' *The Road to Xanadu*, published just three years earlier.[1] Lowes illuminated the ways of Coleridge's mind and, by implication, of all creative imaginations. The results of Coleridge's use of his materials may be profitably compared to de la Mare's, for both shared a passion for narratives of exploration, and de la Mare was sympathetic to many of Coleridge's ideas. De la Mare's materials may have sunk into what Lowes calls "the deep well" of his unconscious, just as Coleridge's did into his. Coleridge's imagination, however, translated the raw material in his unconscious into "Kubla Khan" and "The Ancient Mariner" while de la Mare, using essentially the same kind of material, compiled what is in the final analysis an anthology.

It is perhaps more just to de la Mare to compare his *Desert Islands* to Lowes' work; for *The Road to Xanadu* is an imaginative piece of scholarship with which de la Mare was familiar. The lore in each is as curious, and Lowes' sub-title can well be applied to de la Mare's volume which is a study, in a sense, of the ways of his own imagination. And it is not too unjust to Lowes' scholarship to say that de la Mare's is at least as profound. Of course, their purposes were different. Lowes' was to explore "the ways of the imagination." De la Mare's was to transport his readers on an imaginative voyage; his notes can be read with no reference at all to the text, and in them the reader ranges through all times and climates on all manner of forgotten voyages. Unhappily, however, the reader again concludes that de la Mare felt, as had Matthew Arnold, that "we mortal millions live alone"; for the suggestion is inescapable that we are enisled in the estranging sea of time even as Defoe's Crusoe was in the ocean. This conclusion is evidence that de la Mare shared to some extent the spiritual malaise of the twentieth century, for manifestations of it are to be found in nearly all writers from the turn of the century to the "angry young men" and the theatre of the absurd of recent years.

The realization that man in life is isolated, that "the inmost self of each one of us is a livelong recluse," [2] is the conclusion de la Mare reached in his novels and suggested in his poems and short stories. It would have been a melancholy one had he not also retained his belief that man can live in the imagination. Henry Brocken does so until the time he begins to question, to attempt to comprehend; and the three Mulla-Mulgars have limitless faith in the moonstone, or the imagination, which ultimately leads them to the very doors of the true reality.

The Return represents a turning away from children's stories to adult themes. It and the last two novels can be considered together, for in them the sense of isolation becomes most apparent; and, although the search for reality is pursued in them, they are a more sophisticated investigation of time, dreams, love, and death. As a true representative of his century, in *The Return* de la Mare discovers that time is relative; what is measured by the clock is not necessarily of any consequence. There is in this realization the hint of Blake's idea that it is possible to know "eternity in an hour." Of course, many others before de la Mare had experimented with time, notably Lewis Carroll and George MacDonald, and H. G. Wells on a less metaphysical level. Charles Williams, his contemporary, was to write in *Shadows of Ecstasy* that "Every second is an infinity, once you can enter it." [3] One recalls, of course, the experiments with time in the novels of Dorothy Richardson, Virginia Woolf, and James Joyce.

De la Mare's second discovery in *The Return* is that love is one path by which man can realize the ideal: through the power of love, man truly lives. This is not sexual love, but rather a mutual perception of reality through the power of the imagination. It is, perhaps, in E. M. Forster's terms, the ability to "connect." *At First Sight* is almost a reiteration of this theme; but, instead of abolishing the artificial barrier of time as *The Return* does, the lovers in the latter novel are solidly anchored in time. Both these novels conclude with the parting of the lovers. The reason for the separation in *The Return* is obvious: the lovers were living on three separate planes of consciousness (or of time)—Grisel's, Arthur's, and a third level when they are together. But they cannot remain

[*143*]

on this last level because the other two levels had not merged with the one. Grisel's was more dream than life; Arthur's level was more in life than in dream. These terms can be converted into death (life) and dream (death), if one wishes. Lawford cannot remain on Grisel's level because, as George MacDonald suggests in *Lilith,* one must be spiritually ready to do so. If the term "spiritual" is understood without the usual religious connotations, the reason for Lawford's unreadiness is apparent: he cannot remain with Grisel because his Self is as yet an unknown quantity.

This spiritual unreadiness can be clarified by reference to *Memoirs of a Midget,* de la Mare's statement concerning the reality of the imagination as it applies to knowledge of the Self. The midget has a highly developed sense of identity, but she is incomplete for she lacks what Lawford had found—love. The self is not sufficient unto the Self, the midget learns. She gropes for communication with another imagination through which she can find the Ideal, but the one face of beauty, Fanny, which recalls it to her, she perforce cannot touch. This is not for the reason that Fanny is another woman; they cannot communicate because Fanny lacks imagination and self-knowledge. On the other hand, the midget cannot "connect" with Mr. Anon, her physically repellent lover. She must live to learn, as de la Mare implies she may have, that real beauty is in the spirit, not in the corporeal shell.

Although this explanation may serve to elucidate the reason for Lawford's and Grisel's separation in *The Return,* it does little to explain the separation in *At First Sight* of Cecil and his beloved without some widening of its scope. Cecil's eye-shade and the hints of Miss Simcox's unsavory past must be taken into account. Cecil had never seen anyone, physically or imaginatively, until he looked into the face of his beloved. Then, shortly thereafter, she drowns herself in the river, which can be regarded as a symbol of eternity, or of the imagination, or of the unconscious; for all three terms are related and mean ultimately the same thing to de la Mare. These two events suggest that Cecil was unprepared to live in the imagination for he had never tried to do so before, and that Miss Simcox is also unprepared for she too had lived unimaginatively in the past: she must purge herself of the wounds inflicted by existence. In other words, she is like the suicide, Sabathier; and Cecil is like the midget in that he discovers beauty is not enough.

Conrad, in *Lord Jim* wrote in straightforward language what de la Mare implies: "A man that is born falls into a dream like a man who falls into the sea. If he tries to climb out into the air as inexperienced people endeavor to do, he drowns. . . . The way is to the destructive element submit yourself, and with the exertions of your hands and feet in the water make the deep, deep sea keep you up."

One concludes that de la Mare believed that, although reality is apprehended in the imagination, the quality or duration of the experience depends upon the ability of the imagination to discover both the Self and other selves. Man must live imaginatively, then, but he must "venture into the world without, and the world within." Only with the imagination can man push back the frontiers of the unknown: this was de la Mare's hope and his faith.

It is difficult to suggest the ultimate niche de la Mare will occupy in the cathedral of the British novel. Edward Wagenknecht believes that it will be an important one—near the altar perhaps. E. M. Forster, among others, places him in a dimly lighted chapel, to the side of the nave. Perhaps, however, it will be as Charles Williams suggests about his verse: "In the ever-expanding greatness of English verse it is improbable that more than a score or so of these poems will continue to be generally known; the rest will be reserved for the British Museum Library, special editions, and a few devotees in every generation." [4]

That he was not an anomaly in the modern English novel is apparent. E. M. Forster in 1944 found that de la Mare falls into the group of esoteric novelists as distinguished from the popular group. To two forces, the economic and the psychological, operating upon novelists during this century, Forster attributes the development of the two types. [5] More recently, Horace Gregory suggested that between 1900 and 1950 the loss of faith in scientific and material progress has led to the most significant change in the modern novel; [6] for he finds that, with the impasse reached by the Naturalists, Realism too became less of a goal. [7] Stanley Hopper reached similar conclusions for he maintains that because of the recession of religious faith apparent since the nineteenth century, the artist in recent years has had to find meaning where meaning has ceased to exist, and the quest to do so has become an inward one: "It is a descent into the void of contemporary lostness: a descent in which the moment of time is our only possession, but a time in which there is no fullness. . . ." [8]

The artist's calling, according to Hopper, "is one of alienation and return—if he can make it." [9] He finds in T. S. Eliot and in W. H. Auden two artists who have been able to return. Each of them has resolved the contemporary artist's dilemma for their journeys inward have brought them "to the ultimate mysteries, where ethical and religious understandings take hold." [10] One can conclude that de la Mare was unable to return from the edge of the abyss.

That the sense of isolation pervades modern literature, and that it is at least partly a reflection of the sense of man's alienation from his God that became more apparent as the nineteenth century developed, cannot be doubted. New ways to reality have had to be found; attempts had to be made to cope with the isolation of man from Man. De la Mare's quest is only one among many forms of the twentieth-century search for the meaning of existence. His attempt, as evidenced in his work, was only partially successful. He found, as it were, the scope of the problem; he was able only dimly to perceive its solution. It is revealing that de la Mare believed that his concept of God was similar to Thomas Hardy's, for fundamentally that concept is a Naturalistic one, reflecting the views of a scientific determinist. And although Hardy professed some hope that the human lot may some day be ameliorated, the hope is only dimly expressed. [11]

Being unable to equate his belief in the creative imagination with any metaphysical construct, Walter de la Mare failed to achieve a coherent vision of life. His journey inward brought him, in Stanley Hopper's terms, "to the ultimate mysteries" but the "ethical and religious understandings" he found did not "take hold"—they remained uncertainties. Perhaps he was aware of his failure. Standing outside an edifice of faith, he was able only to grasp the sill and hoist himself up to look through its windows into a world he would never enter. His dying words were: "All these onlookers. . . . I wonder where they all come from." [12] Thus he died essentially himself an onlooker who in all his work expressed the wonder he felt about the mystery of life and death.

Notes and References

Chapter One

1. *Behold, This Dreamer!* (New York, 1939), p. 16.
2. Citations in the text are to "Rupert Brooke and the Intellectual Imagination" reprinted in *Pleasures and Speculations* (London, 1940), pp. 176-77.
3. *Ibid.*, p. 178.
4. *Ibid.*, p. 179.
5. F. C. Bartlett in "Types of Imagination," *Journal of Philosophical Studies*, vol. 3, 1928, pp. 78-85, has a similar method of classification and notes his indebtedness to de la Mare, who could himself have been indebted to Francis Thompson's 1909 essay on Shelley.
6. "Rupert Brooke . . . ," p. 180.
7. Coleridge, *Biographia Literaria*, I.
8. *Early One Morning* (New York, 1935), p. 214.
9. *Behold, This Dreamer!* p. 34.
10. *Ibid.*, p. 27.
11. *Ibid.*, p. 21.
12. *Love* (New York, 1946), p. 21.
13. "Rupert Brooke . . . ," p. 182.
14. "Poetry in Prose," reprinted in *Pleasures and Speculations*, p. 116.
15. T. S. Eliot in an introduction to a new edition of Charles Williams, *All Hallows' Eve* (New York, 1948), xi.
16. "Dream and Wake," *Times Literary Supplement* (December 30, 1915), 498.
17. *Behold, This Dreamer!* note 6, pp. 83-84.
18. *Early One Morning*, p. 133.
19. Carl Jung, *Two Essays on Analytical Psychology* (New York, 1958), p. 76.
20. *Behold, This Dreamer!* note 6, p. 84.
21. *Ibid.*, p. 106.
22. Russell Brain, *Tea with Walter de la Mare* (London, 1957), p. 56.

23. "The Thousand and One," reprinted in *Pleasures and Speculations,* p. 79.

24. *Love,* p. 14.

25. *Love,* cxxiv.

26. "The Supernatural in Nature," *Times Literary Supplement* (November 6, 1919), 618.

27. *The Return* (New York, 1922), p. 253.

28. (New York, n. d.), pp. 178-79.

29. *The Return,* p. 228.

30. In this discussion I have relied primarily on Carl Jung's "Anima and Animus" from his *Two Essays on Analytical Psychology* (New York, 1956), pp. 198-223. For further information on the *anima* concept see his *Intergration of the Personality.* Elizabeth Drew in her very fine study, *T. S. Eliot: The Design of His Poetry* (New York, 1949) applies the *anima* concept to Eliot's *Ash Wednesday,* particularly. So far as I know, however, my application of it to de la Mare was independent of her work.

31. For a remarkable parallel to this, see Jung's "Anima and Animus" where he says that the anima and animus (the female counterpart) "can assume an almost inexhaustible number of shapes . . . their complicated transformations are as rich and strange as the world itself . . . ," pp. 221-22. "In a thousand shapes and disguises she visits us," de la Mare wrote in *Love,* cxxiv.

32. Carl Jung, "Anima and Animus," p. 220.

33. *Ibid.,* p. 222.

Chapter Two

1. *Early One Morning* (New York, 1935), p. 197.

2. *Love* (New York, 1946), p. 47.

3. *Behold, This Dreamer!* (New York, 1939), p. 84.

4. Carl Jung, "On the Relation of Analytic Psychology to Poetic Art," *Contributions to Analytical Psychology* (New York, 1928), p. 227.

5. *Behold, This Dreamer!* pp. 83-84.

6. *Ibid.,* p. 80.

7. *Love,* p. 23. In this connection, see also the long poem "Dreams," from the volume *The Fleeting and Other Poems* in which de la Mare attacks Freudian psychology. Possibly because the poem is a polemic, it is not very good.

8. *Ibid.,* p. 62.

9. *Ibid.,* p. 47.

10. *Behold, This Dreamer!* p. 11.

11. *Ibid.,* p. 97.

12. *Ibid.,* p. 79.
13. Russell Brain, *Tea with Walter de la Mare* (London, 1957), p. 26.
14. *Poetry in Prose,* Wharton Lecture on English Poetry, from the proceedings of The British Academy, XXI (New York, 1937), 45.
15. "Christina Rossetti," *Transactions of The Royal Society of Literature,* New Series VI (Oxford, 1926), p. 100.
16. "Donne," reprinted in *Private View* (London, 1953), p. 159.
17. *Behold, This Dreamer!* p. 14.
18. *Ibid.,* p. 13.
19. *Poetry in Prose,* pp. 151-52.
20. *Behold, This Dreamer!* p. 97.
21. *Ibid.,* p. 41.
22. *Ibid.,* pp. 11-12.
23. *Ibid.,* p. 11.
24. *Ibid.,* p. 79.
25. *Desert Islands and Robinson Crusoe* (New York, 1930), p. 114.
26. *Ibid.,* p. 284.
27. *Love* (London, 1943), lxxvii.
28. Brain, p. 100.
29. *Behold, This Dreamer!* p. 79.
30. *Desert Islands* . . . , p. 72.
31. *Behold, This Dreamer!* pp. 111-12.
32. *Early One Morning,* p. 309.
33. *Love* (London, 1943), cxvii.
34. *Early One Morning,* p. 151.
35. *Love,* p. 64.
36. *Early One Morning,* p. 96.
37. *Ibid.,* p. 13.
38. *Love,* p. 112.
39. *Behold, This Dreamer!* pp. 57-58.

Chapter Three

1. See for example, Edward Wagenknecht, *Cavalcade of the English Novel,* 2nd edition (New York, 1954).
2. It is interesting to contrast the generally well dampened settings in de la Mare's short stories to the arid wastelands of many of his contemporaries. Although de la Mare occasionally used the wasteland symbol—most strikingly in *The Traveller,* his very fine long poem published in 1945—he was no *gerontion:* "an old man in a dry month . . . waiting for rain."
3. See *The Collected Tales of Walter de la Mare,* chosen, and with an introduction by Edward Wagenknecht (New York, 1950).

4. "Creative Criticism" reprinted in *Private View* (London, 1953), p. 4.

5. *Desert Islands and Robinson Crusoe* (New York, 1930), p. 11.

6. *Ibid.*, p. 287.

7. *Behold, This Dreamer!* (New York, 1939), p. 21.

8. *Early One Morning* (New York, 1935), p. 109.

Chapter Four

1. *A Choice of de la Mare's Verse*, selected with an introduction by W. H. Auden (London, 1963), p. 17.

2. The similarity between the early Blake and Dickinson to de la Mare is more than in this one respect. In all three there is the same feeling of wonder, touched, especially in Dickinson and de la Mare, with some rebelliousness.

3. Auden, p. 21.

4. Graham Greene in his contribution to *Tribute to Walter de la Mare on his Seventy-fifth Birthday* (London, 1948), p. 71, is especially strong in his opinion on this point. Greene finds that de la Mare's "obsession with death . . . has never led him to accept—or even to speculate on—the Christian answer. Christianity when it is figured in these stories is like a dead religion. . . . Churches do occur . . . but they are all empty haunted buildings."

5. Victoria Sackville-West, *Walter de la Mare and "The Traveller"* from the Proceedings of the British Academy, XXXIX (London, 1953), 27.

6. Russell Brain in *Tea with Walter de la Mare* (London, 1957), p. 122, records that this stanza was cut with a diamond in a pane of one of the windows at the de la Mare home in Twickenham by Lawrence Whistler.

7. J. B. Priestley, "What Lovely Things," *Tribute to Walter de la Mare*, p. 18.

8. See my chapter "The Shaping Spirit" for further discussion of the "impossible she."

9. Lord Cecil, "The Prose Tales of Walter de la Mare," *Tribute to Walter de la Mare*, p. 64.

10. E. V. Knox, "The Seeing Eye," *Tribute to Walter de la Mare*, p. 57.

11. Brain, pp. 121-22.

Chapter Five

1. Russell Brain, *Tea with Walter de la Mare* (London, 1957), p. 46.

2. See Edward Wagenknecht, *Cavalcade of the English Novel*, 2nd

ed. (New York, 1954), p. 541, note 8, which points to the similarities.

3. See de la Mare, "The Supernatural in Nature," rev. of W. H. Hudson, *The Book of a Naturalist* (London, 1919) *Times Literary Supplement* (November 6, 1919), 617-18; and his "The Novels of Mr. Conrad," rev. of Joseph Conrad, *Chance* (London, 1914) *Times Literary Supplement* (January 15, 1914), 21-22.

4. Grenville MacDonald, *George MacDonald and His Wife* (London, 1924), p. 299.

5. R. L. Mégroz, *Five Novelist-Poets of Today* (London, 1933), p. 27.

6. Grenville MacDonald, p. 298.

7. See de la Mare's studies: *Lewis Carroll* (London, 1932) and "Christina Rossetti," in *Transactions of The Royal Society of Literature*, New Series VI, 1926. See also his introduction to *Come Hither* which indicates the influence of Blake on him.

8. Walter Kaufmann, *Critique of Religion and Philosophy* (New York, 1958), p. 63.

9. *Ibid.*

10. *Love* (London, 1943), cxxxvii.

Chapter Six

1. Forrest Reid, *Walter de la Mare: A Critical Study* (London, 1929), p. 53.

2. Citations in the text are to *Henry Brocken* (London, 1924).

3. George MacDonald, *Phantastes*, 1st edition (London, 1858), reprinted in *The Visionary Novels* with an introduction by W. H. Auden (New York, n. d.).

4. E. M. Forster, *Aspects of the Novel* (New York, 1927), p. 176.

5. R. L. Mégroz, *Walter de la Mare* (London, 1924), p. 268.

6. *Walter de la Mare* (London, 1929), p. 57.

7. Edward Wagenknecht, *Cavalcade of the English Novel*, 2nd edition (New York, 1954), p. 535.

8. Francis Thompson quoted in Mégroz, *Walter de la Mare*, p. 64.

9. Reprinted in *Pleasures and Speculations* (London, 1940). See my discussion of this lecture in the chapter entitled "The Shaping Spirit."

10. *Henry Brocken*, pp. 36-37.

11. *Ibid.*, p. 105.

12. "The Supernatural in Nature," *Times Literary Supplement* (November 6, 1919), 617.

13. *Henry Brocken*, p. 228.

14. *Ibid.*, p. 233.

15. *Ibid.*, p. 234.

16. *Ibid.*, p. 236
17. *Ibid.*, p. 237.
18. "Love in Fiction," *Times Literary Supplement* (October 30, 1918), 490.
19. "What man has wholly forgiven Criseyde?" de la Mare asked in *Love* (London, 1943).
20. "The Mask of Transciency," *Times Literary Supplement* (June 12, 1919), 323.
21. Russell Brain, *Tea with Walter de la Mare* (London, 1957), p. 67.
22. *Ibid.*, pp. 66, 78, 88.
23. *Ibid.*, p. 88.
24. *Henry Brocken*, p. 234.
25. *Behold, This Dreamer!* (London, 1939), p. 83.
26. John Freeman, *English Portraits and Essays* (London, 1924), p. 99.
27. Llewellyn Jones, *First Impressions* (London, 1925), p. 133.
28. *Henry Brocken*, p. 14. Note also de la Mare's discussion of the limerick about the "Old Man in a Boat," in *Lewis Carroll* (London, 1932), p. 16.
29. *Behold, This Dreamer!* p. 65.
30. De la Mare refers to this phenomenon in *The Return*, p. 200: "The howl of a dog turns the midnight into a Brocken. . . ."
31. Brain, p. 65.
32. *Behold, This Dreamer!* p. 101.
33. Mégroz, *Walter de la Mare*, p. 4 quotes de la Mare: "Don't you think that the essential truth for each one of us is in our individual imagination?"
34. Brain, pp. 36-37. See also de la Mare's mention of the same experience in *Behold, This Dreamer!* p. 63.
35. *Ibid.*, p. 38.
36. Virginia Rice, "On Not Interviewing Walter de la Mare," *Bookman* (September, 1922), 50.
37. Mégroz, *Walter de la Mare*, p. 5.
38. *Love* (London, 1943), cxxxiii-cxxxiv.
39. *Behold, This Dreamer!* p. 65.
40. *Love*, ccxvi.
41. Joyce Cary, *Art and Reality* (New York, 1958).
42. William Van O'Connor, *Forms of Modern Fiction* (Oxford, 1948), p. 3.
43. Walter Kaufmann, *Critique of Religion and Philosophy* (New York, 1958), p. 66.
44. *Ibid.*

45. T. S. Eliot, "Tradition and the Individual Talent," *The Sacred Wood,* 7th ed. (London, 1950), pp. 49-51.
46. Frank Thilly, *A History of Philosophy,* revised by Ledger Wood (New York, 1951), pp. 471-72.

Chapter Seven

1. Citations in the text are to *The Three Royal Monkeys* (London, 1945).
2. Forrest Reid, *Walter de la Mare* (London, 1929), p. 112.
3. *Ibid.,* p. 111.
4. R. L. Mégroz, *Walter de la Mare* (London, 1924), p. 75.
5. R. L. Mégroz, *Five Novelist-Poets of Today* (London, 1933), p. 27.
6. Reid, *Walter de la Mare,* p. 124.
7. "Poetry in Prose," reprinted in *Pleasures and Speculations* (London, 1940), p. 12.
8. Reid, *Walter de la Mare,* p. 125.
9. G. K. Chesterton, "Walter de la Mare," *Fortnightly Review* (July, 1932), 50.
10. "Mystihood" is a term borrowed from Mark Schorer's *William Blake* (New York, 1946), p. 51, and is defined as "partial mysticism." On the distinction between symbolism and allegory W. H. Auden's discussion of allegory, cited later in this chapter, is helpful.
11. Mégroz, *Five Novelist-Poets of Today,* p. 27.
12. De la Mare often used the word "paradise," which has fewer religious connotations than "heaven," a word he seldom employed.
13. Edward Wagenknecht, *Cavalcade of the English Novel,* 2nd ed. (New York, 1954), p. 536.
14. *Ibid.*
15. W. H. Auden, in the introduction to George MacDonald, *The Visionary Novels: Lilith and Phantastes* (New York, n. d.), vi.
16. *The Three Royal Monkeys,* p. 110.
17. *Ibid.,* p. 119.
18. Russell Brain, *Tea with Walter de la Mare* (London 1957), p. 44.
19. *The Three Royal Monkeys,* p. 268.
20. *Ibid.* See the echo of this thought in de la Mare's *Desert Islands and Robinson Crusoe* (London, 1930), p. 205: "Dreams remembered on waking that continue to haunt the mind as if with an assurance of some secret meaning are unusual. . . ." Note, also, that de la Mare's use of "forest" here echoes Blake's—the "forest" is the vegetable world of error. Only by exercise of the imagination can one see beyond the forest to the ultimate.

21. Grenville MacDonald, *George MacDonald and His Wife* (London, 1924), p. 543.

22. George MacDonald, *The Visionary Novels*, p. 31.

23. *Ibid.*, p. 257.

24. Charles Williams, *Shadows of Ecstasy* (London, 1931), p. 192.

25. *The Three Royal Monkeys*, p. 271. De la Mare may have borrowed the leopard symbol from emblematic literature in which the leopard is a symbol of Christ. (See Eliot's "Gerontion" and "Ash Wednesday" for a contemporary use of this symbol.) In de la Mare, however, the symbol seems to have scant reference to Christ although there are suggestions of resurrectional connotations. MacDonald also employed the symbol, but in *Lilith*, for example, it seems to connote evil; at least, destruction.

26. *The Three Royal Monkeys*, p. 266.

27. *Ibid.*, p. 267.

28. *Ibid.*, p. 212.

Chapter Eight

1. Citations in the text are to *The Return* (New York, 1922).

2. J. B. Priestley, "Mr. de la Mare's Imagination," *London Mercury* (May, 1924), 34.

3. Kenneth Hopkins, *Walter de la Mare*, British Council and National Book League (London, 1953), p. 17.

4. Forrest Reid, *Walter de la Mare* (London, 1929), p. 130.

5. *Ibid.*, p. 131.

6. Edward Wagenknecht, *Cavalcade of the English Novel*, 2nd ed. (New York, 1954), p. 537.

7. R. L. Mégroz, *Walter de la Mare* (London, 1924), p. 143.

8. Reid, p. 139.

9. *Ibid.*

10. Note the similarity of the experience portrayed here to that in de la Mare's *Ding Dong Bell* (New York, 1924), pp. 70-76.

11. *The Return*, p. 290.

12. "Love in Fiction," *Times Literary Supplement* (October 30, 1918), 490.

13. *Times Literary Supplement* (November 6, 1919), 618.

14. *The Return*, p. 136.

15. *Ibid.*, p. 141.

16. *Ibid.*, p. 143.

17. *Ibid.*, p. 201.

18. *Ibid.*, p. 205.

19. *Ibid.*, p. 228.

20. *Ibid.*, p. 229.

21. *Ibid.*, p. 231.
22. *Ibid.*, p. 239.
23. *Ibid.*, p. 253.
24. *Ibid.*, p. 125. "Widderstone" may be a play on the word "Widdershins"—to reverse, to turn topsy-turvy.
25. *Ibid.*
26. John Atkins, *Walter de la Mare: An Exploration* (London, 1947), p. 8.
27. *Ding Dong Bell* (London, 1924).
28. Russell Brain, *Tea with Walter de la Mare* (London, 1957), p. 49.
29. *The Return*, p. 153.
30. *Ibid.*, p. 136.
31. *Ibid.*, p. 167.
32. *Ibid.*, p. 168.
33. *Ibid.*, p. 171.
34. *Ibid.*, p. 141.
35. *Ibid.*, p. 128.
36. *Behold, This Dreamer!* (London, 1939), p. 60.
37. *The Return*, p. 128.
38. *Ibid.*, p. 129.
39. *Behold, This Dreamer!* pp. 38-39. The metaphor of "The Chinese nest of boxes" often appears in de la Mare's work.
40. *Ibid.*, p. 40.
41. Brain, pp. 35-36.
42. Grenville MacDonald, *George MacDonald and His Wife* (London, 1924), p. 403.
43. George MacDonald, *The Visionary Novels* (New York, n. d.), p. 92.
44. *The Return*, p. 137. Note also a similar idea in T. S. Eliot's *The Cocktail Party*.
45. *Behold, This Dreamer!* p. 65.
46. *The Return*, p. 234.
47. *Ibid.*
48. *Ibid.*, p. 239. Compare this to a similar experience de la Mare wrote of in *Come Hither* (New York, 1957), ix.
49. *The Return*, p. 236.
50. *Ibid.*, p. 238.
51. *Ibid.*, p. 245.
52. *Ibid.*, p. 246.
53. *Ibid.*, p. 248.
54. *Ibid.*, pp. 248-49.
55. *Ibid.*, p. 250.

56. *Ibid.*, p. 257.
57. *Ibid.*, p. 252.
58. *Ibid.*, p. 253.
59. Brain, p. 90.
60. *Ibid.*, p. 62.
61. *Ibid.*, p. 23.
62. *Behold, This Dreamer!* p. 112.
63. Sir James George Frazer, *The Golden Bough,* abridged ed. (New York, 1949), pp. 189-94.
64. Brain, pp. 48, 63.
65. *Behold, This Dreamer!* p. 13.
66. *Ibid.*, p. 108.
67. *Ibid.*, p. 104.
68. Brain, p. 60.
69. *The Return,* p. 14.
70. *Ibid.*, p. 54.
71. *Ibid.*, p. 221.
72. *Ibid.*, pp. 107, 266.
73. *Ibid.*, p. 137.
74. *Ibid.*, p. 15.
75. See *Memoirs of a Midget.*
76. *Love* (London, 1943).
77. *Ibid.*, cxvii.
78. *Ibid.*, lxxiv.

Chapter Nine

1. Citations in the text are to *Memoirs of a Midget* (New York, 1941).
2. Russell Brain in *Tea with Walter de la Mare* (London, 1957), p. 20, indicates that a small bust of Hypnos was one of de la Mare's possessions.
3. *Memoirs,* p. 3.
4. Joseph Collins, *Taking the Literary Pulse* (New York, 1924), p. 65.
5. Sir James George Frazer. *The Growth of Plato's Ideal Theory* (London, 1930), p. 56.
6. E. M. Forster, *Aspects of the Novel* (New York, 1927), p. 160.
7. George MacDonald, *The Visionary Novels: Lilith and Phantastes* (New York, n. d.), p. 265.
8. "Books and Reading," *Living Age* (March 22, 1919), 744.
9. For this opinion see Atkins, *Walter de la Mare* (London, 1947), p. 29.
10. *Memoirs,* pp. 304-5.

11. *Ibid.*, p. 181.
12. *Ibid.*, p. 6.
13. *Ibid.*, p. 8.
14. *Ibid.*, p. 27.
15. *Desert Islands and Robinson Crusoe* (London, 1930), p. 43.
16. Grenville MacDonald, *George MacDonald and His Wife* (London, 1924), p. 550. There are suggestions here too of St. John of the Cross and William Blake. Another sense might be the kinesthetic; this, with intuition would equal seven.
17. *Memoirs*, p. 41.
18. *Ibid.*, p. 76.
19. *Ibid.*, p. 221.
20. *Ibid.*, p. 156.
21. Atkins, p. 43.
22. See my chapter on "Dreams and the Dreamer" for a discussion of de la Mare's opinions regarding Freudian psychology.
23. *Memoirs*, p. 96.
24. *Ibid.*, p. 98. See also the Arthur Lawford-Nicholas Sabathier relationship with Grisel in *The Return*.
25. See *Behold, This Dreamer!* (London, 1939), p. 80, for a reiteration of this point.
26. *Memoirs*, p. 107.
27. *Ibid.*, p. 100.
28. *Ibid.*, p. 339.
29. *Ibid.*, p. 340. The similarity between the supposedly "normal" Fanny Bowater and the central character in Pär Lagerkuist's *The Dwarf* is startling.
30. *Ibid.*, p. 341.
31. *Ibid.*, p. 98.
32. R. L. Mégroz. *Five Novelist-Poets of Today* (London, 1933), p. 54.
33. Brain, pp. 25, 44.
34. *Memoirs*, p. 107.
35. *Ibid.*, p. 165.
36. *Ibid.*, p. 191.
37. *Ibid.*, p. 162.
38. *Ibid.*, p. 242. This attitude toward names is similar to that held by Herbert Herbert in *The Return*.
39. Lewis Carroll, *Alice's Adventures in Wonderland and Through the Looking Glass* (New York, 1946), p. 198.
40. See for example, Brain, pp. 36-37, and *Behold, This Dreamer!* p. 63.
41. *Memoirs*, p. 259.

42. *Ibid.*, p. 260.
43. *Ibid.*, p. 378.
44. *Ibid.*, p. 8.
45. *Ibid.*, p. 340.
46. *Ibid.*, p. 263.
47. *Ibid.*, p. 107.
48. *Ibid.*, p. 210.
49. *Ibid.*, p. 22. For the record of a similar experience de la Mare had as a child see *Early One Morning* (New York, 1935), p. 261.
50. "The Reading of Contemporary Poetry," *Living Age* (June 28, 1919), 792.
51. *Memoirs*, p. 240.
52. *Ibid.*, p. 223.
53. *Behold, This Dreamer!* pp. 27-28.
54. "The Supernatural in Nature," *Times Literary Supplement* (November 6, 1919), 618.
55. *Behold, This Dreamer!* p. 84.
56. *Memoirs*, p. 261. One is reminded of the last line of "Prufrock": "Till human voices wake us and we drown."
57. *Ibid.*, p. 108.
58. *Ibid.*, p. 262.
59. *Ibid.*
60. *Ibid.*, pp. 378-79.

Chapter Ten

1. Walter de la Mare, *Love* (London, 1943), liii.
2. Citations in the text are to "At First Sight," reprinted in *On the Edge* (London, 1930). Although this can hardly be called a novel in any sense of the word, it is considered as one here, because that is what de la Mare labeled it. His reason might have been that it is in essence a novel; certainly the bare bones, upon which incidents and characters could have been hung to flesh it out, are here.
3. De la Mare in *Ding Dong Bell* (New York, 1924), p. 7, shows another debt to Hawthorne.
4. "At First Sight," p. 127.
5. *Ibid.*, p. 122.
6. *Ibid.*, p. 128.
7. *Ibid.*, p. 154.
8. *Ibid.*, p. 192.
9. *Ibid.*
10. *Ibid.*, p. 198.
11. *The Return* (New York, 1922), p. 253.
12. *Ibid.*, p. 196.

13. *Ibid.*, p. 200.
14. *Love* (London, 1943), cxxxix.
15. "Christina Rossetti," *Transactions of the Royal Society of Literature,* New Series VI (Oxford, 1926), p. 101.
16. *Love*, cxxxvii.

Chapter Eleven

1. John Livingstone Lowes, *The Road to Xanadu* (New York, 1927).
2. *Desert Islands and Robinson Crusoe* (London, 1930), p. 27.
3. Charles Williams, *Shadows of Ecstasy* (London, 1931), p. 202.
4. Charles Williams, *Poetry at Present* (Oxford, 1930), pp. 94-95.
5. E. M. Forster, *The Development of English Prose Between 1918 and 1939* (Glasgow, 1945).
6. Horace Gregory, "Mutations of Belief in the Contemporary Novel" in *Spiritual Problems in Contemporary Literature,* Stanley Romaine Hopper, ed. (New York & London, 1952), p. 39.
7. *Ibid.*, p. 40.
8. Stanley Romaine Hopper, "The Problem of Moral Isolation in Contemporary Literature" in *Spiritual Problems in Contemporary Literature,* Stanley Romaine Hopper, ed. (New York & London, 1952), p. 154.
9. *Ibid.*, p. 153.
10. *Ibid.*, p. 167.
11. Joseph Warren Beach, *The Concept of Nature in Nineteenth Century English Poetry,* 2nd ed. (New York, 1956), pp. 503-21.
12. Russell Brain, *Tea with Walter de la Mare* (London, 1957), p. 157.

Selected Bibliography

PRIMARY SOURCES

In this list of the works of Walter de la Mare, I have included only what I believe to be his major publications. Many of his poems and short stories were first published separately only to be later included in collections. I have ignored the separate editions, hoping that by listing the collections and their first dates of publication, the reader who wishes to discover the most significant publications will be best served. The works are listed, each in its category, chronologically, in order of publication.

I. Bibliographies:

An invaluable source of bibliographical information regarding first and variant editions of books by de la Mare, his contributions to other authors' books and to periodicals, and foreign editions of his works is: *Walter de la Mare:* A check list prepared on the occasion of an exhibition of his books and manuscripts at The National Book League, April 20 to May 19, 1956, published for The National Book League at The University Press, Cambridge, in 1956.
Other useful sources of bibliographical information are:

CLARK, LEONARD. "A Handlist of the Writings in Book Form (1902-53) of Walter de la Mare" in *Studies in Bibliography,* Papers of the Bibliographical Society of the University of Virginia, Fredson Bowers, ed. Charlottesville, Virginia: Bibliographical Society of the University of Virginia, 1953.
HOPKINS, KENNETH. *Walter de la Mare.* Published for The British Council and The National Book League: Writers and Their Work, No. 36. London: Longmans, Green & Co. rev. ed. 1957.

II. Poetry:

Songs of Childhood. London: Longmans, Green & Co., 1902.
Poems. London: Murray, 1906.
The Listeners and Other Poems. London: Constable, 1912.

A Child's Day. A book of rhymes. London: Constable, 1912.
Peacock Pie. A Book of rhymes. London: Constable, 1913.
Motley and Other Poems. London: Constable, 1918.
Poems 1901 to 1918. London: Constable, 1920.
Down-a down-derry: A book of Fairy Poems. London: Constable, 1922.
Stuff and Nonsense and So On. London: Constable, 1922.
Poems for Children. London: Constable, 1930.
The Fleeting and Other Poems. London: Constable, 1933.
Poems 1919 to 1934. London: Constable, 1935.
This Year, Next Year. London: Faber, 1937.
Memory and Other Poems. London: Constable, 1938.
Collected Poems. London: Faber, 1942.
Collected Rhymes and Verses. London: Faber, 1944.
The Burning Glass and other poems . . . including The Traveller. New York: Viking Press, 1945.
Winged Chariot. London: Faber, 1951.
O Lovely England and Other Poems. London: Faber, 1953.

III.   The Short Stories: Collections

Story and Rhyme. A selection . . . chosen by the author. New York: Dutton; London: Dent [1921].
The Riddle and Other Stories. London: Selwyn and Blount, 1923.
Ding Dong Bell. London: Selwyn and Blount, 1924.
Broomsticks and Other Tales. London: Constable, 1925.
The Connoisseur and Other Stories. London: Collins, 1926.
Told Again: Traditional Tales. Oxford: Blackwell, 1927.
Stories From The Bible. London: Faber and Gwyer, 1929.
On The Edge. London: Faber, 1930.
The Lord Fish. London: Faber [1933].
The Wind Blows Over. London: Faber, 1936.
The Best Stories of Walter de la Mare. Selected by the author. London: Faber, 1942.
The Magic Jacket and Other Stories. London: Faber, 1943.
The Scarecrow and Other Stories. London: Faber, 1945.
The Dutch Cheese and Other Stories. London: Faber, 1946.
Collected Stories for Children. Selected by the author. London: Faber, 1947.
A Beginning and Other Stories. London: Faber, 1955.

IV.   The Novels

Henry Brocken. His travels and adventures in the rich, strange, scarce-imaginable regions of romance. London: John Murray, 1904.

[162]

Bibliography

The Return. London: Arnold, 1910.
The Three Mulla-Mulgars. London: Duckworth, 1910. Later published
     by Faber as *The Three Royal Monkeys* or *The Three Mulla-
     Mulgars,* 1935.
Memoirs of a Midget. London: Collins, 1921.
At First Sight: A Novel. New York: Crosby Gaige, 1928; reprinted in
     On The Edge. London: Faber, 1930.

V. Play:

Crossings: A fairy play. London: Beaumont Press, 1921.

VI. Anthologies:

Come Hither. A collection of rhymes and poems for the young of all
     ages. London: Constable, 1923.
Desert Islands and Robinson Crusoe. London: Faber, 1930.
Early One Morning in the Spring. Chapters on Children and Child-
     hood as it is revealed in particular in early memories and early
     writings. London: Faber, 1935.
Behold, This Dreamer! Of reverie, night, sleep, dream, love-dreams,
     nightmare, death, the unconscious, the imagination, divination,
     the artist, and kindred subjects. London: Faber, 1939.
Love. London: Faber, 1943.

VII. Essays and Lectures:

Rupert Brooke and the Intellectual Imagination. London: Sedgwick &
     Jackson, 1919.
"Books and Reading," *Living Age* (March 22, 1919), 744-47.
"The Reading of Contemporary Poetry," *Living Age* (June 28, 1919),
     791-95.
"Christina Rossetti," *Transactions of The Royal Society of Literature.*
     G. K. Chesterton, ed. New Series VI. Oxford, 1926.
Poetry in Prose. Wharton Lecture in English Poetry, British Academy,
     1935. From the Proceedings of The British Academy. XXI. Ox-
     ford University Press, 1935.
Pleasures and Speculations. London: Faber, 1940. A collection of es-
     says on various subjects.
"A Quiet Life," Giff Edmonds Memorial Lecture. *Transactions of The
     Royal Society of Literature.* Gordon Bottomley, ed. New Series
     XX. Oxford, 1943.
Private View. London: Faber, 1953. Another collection of essays.
Walter de la Mare wrote scores of essays and reviews for *The Times
     Literary Supplement.* The best source of information regarding
     them is Edward Wagenknecht's "Walter de la Mare, Book Re-

viewer" which includes a bibliography of reviews by de la Mare. The article is to be found in the *Boston University Studies in English* (Winter, 1955-1956), 211-39.

SECONDARY SOURCES

In this list are included works by other authors cited in this study, with annotations concerning the ones important to an understanding of de la Mare.

ATKINS, JOHN. *Walter de la Mare: An Exploration*. London: C. & J. Temple, 1947. A brief but suggestive analysis.

BARTLETT, F. C. "Types of Imagination," *Journal of Philosophical Studies*, III (1928), 78-85. A discussion of the imagination; admits an indebtedness to de la Mare.

BEACH, JOSEPH WARREN. *The Concept of Nature in Nineteenth-Century English Poetry*. 2nd. Ed. New York: Pageant, 1956.

BRAIN, RUSSELL. *Tea with Walter de la Mare*. London: Faber, 1957. An informal record of conversations between de la Mare and the eminent neurologist. Valuable for the light it throws on de la Mare's thinking during his last years.

CARY, JOYCE. *Art and Reality: Ways of the Creative Imagination*. New York: Harper, 1958.

CECIL, LORD DAVID. *The English Poets*. London: Collins, 1942. A perceptive reader of de la Mare's poetry.

CHESTERTON, G. K. "Walter de la Mare," *Fortnightly Review* (July, 1932), 47-53.

CHURCH, RICHARD. *Eight for Immortality*. London: Dent, 1941.

————. "Walter de la Mare," *Fortnightly Review* (March, 1940), 304-11.

COATS, R. H. "The World of Walter de la Mare," *Fortnightly Review* (October, 1927), 483-91.

COLLINS, JOSEPH. *Taking the Literary Pulse: Psychological Studies of Life and Letters*. New York: Doran, 1924.

DUFFIN, HENRY CHARLES. *Walter de la Mare: A Study of His Poetry*. London: Sedgwick and Jackson, 1949. A pioneer work insofar as this is the first book-length study devoted to de la Mare's poetry. Somewhat effusive and repetitious.

ELIOT, T. S. "Tradition and the Individual Talent," *The Sacred Wood: Essays on Poetry and Criticism*. 7th ed. New York: Barnes and Noble, 1950.

FORSTER, E. M. *Aspects of the Novel*. New York: Harcourt, 1927. Most important for placing de la Mare's novels in the context of the British tradition.

Bibliography

————. *The Development of English Prose Between 1918 and 1939.* Glasgow: Jackson, 1945. Another important assessment of de la Mare.

FRAZER, SIR JAMES GEORGE. *The Golden Bough: A Study in Magic and Religion.* One volume, abridged ed. New York: Macmillan, 1949.

————. *The Growth of Plato's Ideal Theory: An Essay.* New York: Macmillan, 1930.

FREEMAN, JOHN. *English Portraits and Essays.* London: Bookman, 1924.

GINGRICH, JOHN P. *An Immortality for Its Own Sake: A Study of the Concept of Poetry in the Writings of Charles Williams.* A Dissertation. Washington, D.C., 1954.

HOPKINS, KENNETH. *Walter de la Mare.* British Council and National Book League, Writers and Their Work Series, No. 36. London: Longmans, Green, 1953. An excellent but too brief overview of de la Mare's work. Includes bibliography.

HOPPER, STANLEY ROMAINE, ed. *Spiritual Problems in Contemporary Literature: A Series of Addresses and Discussions.* Religion and Civilization Series. New York: Harper, 1952. Helpful in understanding any modern writer.

JONES, LLEWELLYN. *First Impressions: Essays on Poetry, Criticism, and Prosody.* New York: Knopf, 1925.

————. "Walter de la Mare: Poet of Tishnar," *Bookman* (July, 1923), 528-32.

JUNG, CARL. G. "On the Relation of Analytical Psychology to Poetic Art," *Contributions to Analytical Psychology.* Trans. H. G. and Cary F. Baynes, in *International Library of Psychology, Philosophy and Scientific Method,* vol. 60. New York: Harcourt, 1928. Acquaintance with Jung is indispensable to the understanding of contemporary literature.

————. *Two Essays on Analytical Psychology.* Trans. R. F. C. Hull. New York: Meridian Books, 1956.

KAUFMANN, WALTER. *Critique of Religion and Philosophy.* New York: Harper, 1958.

LOWES, JOHN LIVINGSTON. *The Road to Xanadu: A Study in the Ways of the Imagination.* New York: Houghton, 1927. Important to any student of the imagination.

MACDONALD, GEORGE. *The Visionary Novels: Lilith and Phantastes.* Anne Freemantle, ed.; with an introduction by W. H. Auden. New York: Noonday, 1954. Both novels are outstanding representatives of the dream, or visionary, novel.

MACDONALD, GRENVILLE. *George MacDonald and His Wife,* with an introduction by G. K. Chesterton. London: Dial, 1924. An important source concerning MacDonald which also throws some light on de la Mare's imagination.

MÉGROZ, R. L. *Five Novelist-Poets of Today*. London: Joiner, 1933. Mr. Mégroz, a friend of de la Mare's, examines de la Mare's life and work in this and the following study.

————. *Walter de la Mare: A Biographical and Critical Study*. London: Hodder & Stoughton, 1924. The first long critical study. Useful for biographical information.

O'CONNOR, WILLIAM VAN, ed. *Forms of Modern Fiction: Essays Collected in Honor of Joseph Warren Beach*. Oxford, 1948.

REID, FORREST. *Walter de la Mare: A Critical Study*. London: Faber, 1929. An important study of de la Mare.

RICE, VIRGINIA. "On Not Interviewing Walter de la Mare," *Bookman* (September, 1922), 50-52.

SACKVILLE-WEST, VICTORIA. "Walter de la Mare and 'The Traveller,' " *Proceedings of the British Academy*. XXXIX (London, 1953).

SWINNERTON, FRANK. *The Georgian Scene: A Literary Panorama*. New York: Farrar, 1934.

TAYLOR, ALEXANDER. *The White Knight: A Study of C. L. Dodgson (Lewis Carroll)*. London: Clark, Irwin, 1952. A most suggestive reading of an author whose influence on de la Mare was profound.

THILLY, FRANK. *A History of Philosophy*. Revised by Ledger Wood. New York: Holt, Rinehart and Winston, 1951.

THOMAS, DYLAN. "Walter de la Mare as a Prose Writer," *Quite Early One Morning*. London: Dent, 1954; also New York: New Directions, 1954. Thomas' own reputation makes whatever he has to say significant. His appraisal here, though brief, is fair.

Tribute to Walter de la Mare on His Seventy-Fifth Birthday. Dr. W. R. Bett, ed. London: Faber, 1948. A rare edition; with articles by Graham Greene, Lord David Cecil and others.

WAGENKNECHT, EDWARD. *Cavalcade of the English Novel*. 2nd ed. New York: Holt, Rinehart and Winston, 1954. Mr. Wagenknecht is enthusiastic about the novels, and suggests that in the future the novel will follow the direction pointed to by them.

————. "Walter de la Mare, Book Reviewer," with a Bibliography of reviews by Walter de la Mare. *Boston University Studies in English*, I (Winter, 1955-1956), 211-39. The only appraisal of de la Mare's contribution to a rather ephemeral kind of literary endeavor. The bibliography is invaluable.

WILLIAMS, CHARLES. *All Hallows' Eve*, with an introduction by T. S. Eliot. New York: Pellegrini & Cudahy. 1948. Williams' novels and his criticism provide necessary insights into de la Mare's work. Eliot's introduction touches on de la Mare.

————. *The English Poetic Mind.* Oxford: 1932.

————. *The Greater Trumps,* with a preface by William **Lindsay** Gresham. New York: Pellegrini & Cudahy, 1950.

————. *Poetry at Present.* Oxford: 1930.

————. *Reason and Beauty in the Poetic Mind.* Oxford: 1933.

————. *Shadows of Ecstasy.* London: Gollancz, 1931.

————. *War in Heaven.* London: Gollancz, 1930.

Index